BUY
OR SELL
YOUR HOME

Lucy Chuo

FOR SALE

LEGAL ESSENTIALS
FOR
SMOOTHER PROPERTY TRANSACTIONS

To
Sping Family,
Thank you so much for
taking care of me many
years ago. Hope you enjoy
reading my book with fond
memories and love Lucy x

LAWUNDERSTOOD

First Published in 2017 in Great Britain by Law Understood Ltd, The Big Peg, 120 Vyse Street, Birmingham, West Midlands, England, B18 6NF

Cataloguing in Publication Data is available from the British Library.

ISBN 978-0-9934961-4-1

Printed and bound in the United Kingdom
Printed by TJ International, Padstow, Cornwall
Cover illustration by Steve Norton - www.stevenorton.co.uk

www.lawunderstood.com

DEDICATION

This book is dedicated to my late mother, Magdalen Wong
Suok Ting 黄雪珍 , and father, Chuo Kwong Chuang 朱光铨
who gave me the best start in life by instilling in me their
values: a strong work ethic coupled with ambition; a sense of
self-worth and empowerment; and last, but by no means least,
integrity.

ACKNOWLEDGEMENTS

With grateful appreciation to all those who have helped in the creation of Law Understood's Buy or Sell your Home, Legal Essentials for Smoother Property Transaction.

To my late Mother, Magdalen Wong Suok Ting, and Father, Chuo Kwong Chuang, who gave me the opportunity to attend the Stella Maris Convent in North Devon at the age of 7, giving me the best educational start, and who instilled in me from an early age the values of working hard, staying determined and always believing in myself. Equally, I would like to thank all my siblings - Annie, Olivia, Susan and John for their continued support and encouragement.

To all of the contributors of this book, namely: Andrew, Cindi, Daniel, Malcolm, Mathew, Michael, Paul, Philip, and Robert (all their profiles are listed at the back of this book). I give thanks to all of them for their enthusiasm and feedback, and for the generous sharing of their invaluable knowledge and experiences.

I would like to thank Steve, our graphic designer, for the creative book's design and cover. I also give thanks to David and Liz for helping us format our book in a professional and timely manner, as well as Chris for his patience in helping us create our Kindle version and uploading this book to Amazon.

Special thanks go to my energetic legal team led and directed by Sean, my executive assistant. Thank you also to Joey and Yavor for their editing skills and for helping to develop this book, as well as their tireless work in arranging the interviews with the contributors.

TABLE OF CONTENTS

INTRODUCTION

For most individuals, the process of buying or selling a property can be both a daunting and an exciting prospect. You may be a young couple wishing to purchase your first home together, a sizeable family seeking to sell and relocate to a something bigger, or perhaps you are even interested in buying a property and then deriving income through rent.

There is a myriad of reasons as to why one might consider buying or selling a property. The residential property turnover is gradually increasing, with The Office for National Statistics[1] reporting 3,784,988 residential property sales in England and Wales for 2016. The latest data shows that the residential property sales for the first three quarters of 2016 are up 5.9% compared with the sales in the first three quarters of 2015. As a result, 2016 has been the year with the most residential real estate purchases since the 2008 financial crisis.

Another definitive characteristic of the residential real estate market in England and Wales is the rapidly increasing house prices. The median residential purchase price in London for 2015 was approximately £386,000, with the median price for 2016 so far being around £426,000. This is an increase in prices of approximately 10% over just one year. This trend is observed throughout the country, with median prices in England and Wales having increased from approximately £202,000 for 2015, to around £213,000 for 2016 – an increase of about 5%. This increase in prices is a possible reason for the increases in residential property purchases. Many are afraid that delaying purchasing their home by a year or two might result in substantially higher prices. This trend of price increase might be affected by the departure of the UK from the EU. However, the latest data shows that in the third quarter of 2016, immediately after the membership referendum, median residential real estate prices increased, compared to the second quarter of 2016. Of course, making an accurate prediction about the exact future of housing prices is impossible, with the consequences of Brexit yet to unfold fully.

The statistics show that buying residential property is becoming an increasingly common prospect. Regardless of the trends, it remains a fact that the process of buying or selling property is not fully understood by most people. Those without the necessary experience often have to pay a great price in terms of stress and financial expenses. The process of conveyancing is quite complex, because it includes numerous steps and involves multiple parties.

It is the aim of this book to present an easy-to-understand guide to the challenges of buying or selling a residential property. This book explains with clarity the general steps of the process, from finding an experienced estate agent, explaining the mortgage requirements, ordering the right searches, examining the title documents, and to completing the necessary forms. All that is left for you to do is to pick up the keys to your new property!

This book we will only be addressing residential property sales and purchases in the UK of registered land. This is because most of the properties you will come across will have been registered and the conveyancing process for unregistered land may differ. It is also important to note that each property transaction is unique and although we aim to provide as much detail on the process as possible, the specifics of your case could fall outside of the scope of this book.

In order to help you find the information you need, references to important forms, reports, databases, tools and agencies can be found throughout this publication. You will find numbers in superscript referring to entries in the Reference section at the back of the book in order to access the full links to the corresponding entries.

CHAPTER ONE
Finance, Location, Surveys and Insurance

Most people decide to buy a property at some stage of their lives. For most of us, this is the largest purchase we will ever make. As a result, financial planning is one of the most important things to consider when preparing to buy a property. The process of buying or selling a property may generally take around 8 weeks, however this is not set in stone: delays or unexpected events can prolong that period considerably. As such, it is important to keep a track of both planned and unexpected expenses.

In this book, we will use the collective term "property" to refer to a wide range of residential real estate: houses, apartments, villas, bungalows, lodges, and any other type of residential real estate that you might be able to purchase on the market. Generally, the process of purchasing/selling any of those properties is similar.

Some expenses you may need to consider include:
» The deposit for the property you are intending to buy;
» The repayments you will make in relation to your mortgage arrangement;
» The cost of hiring a mortgage broker and/or an estate agent;
» The cost of having a survey done;
» The cost of buildings insurance;

» The cost of moving home;
» Legal representative's fees;
» The cost of conducting Searches; and
» Stamp Duty Land Tax.

This long list of expenses might seem intimidating at first sight. However, this book sets out the different expenses usually encountered and explains whether they are mandatory requirements or option precautions.

1. FINANCING THE PURCHASE OF YOUR PROPERTY

The first step is to ask yourself if you can afford to buy the property you want. In doing so, you are basically calculating how much money you can personally contribute towards the purchase and how much you must borrow if required. Some fortunate people may be able to purchase their properties outright, however we do not all have pockets or purses so profound. Homeowners might be able to finance the purchase by selling their existing home, which is called a linked chain of sale and purchase. However, very often property buyers need to apply to a lender (i.e. bank, building society) for a mortgage.

a. MORTGAGES

Suppose that you want to borrow money from a bank or a building society to purchase a property. They provide loans at an interest, meaning that you will have to make repayments to pay off your debt as well as the interest accrued.

A mortgage is a loan for a fixed period that you, the borrower, must pay interest on. As part of this arrangement, the lender acquires a conditional right of ownership over your property. If you continue to make your payments on time, the lender has no right to take possession of your mortgaged property. In addition, this conditional right will be extinguished once you have discharged your mortgage. The mortgage discharge occurs when you fulfil your obligation to the lender.

However, if you fail to make a payment on time or pay less than what is owed according to your arrangement, your mortgage will go into default, which means that the lender has the legal right to take possession of your mortgaged property. If this happens or if you are struggling to make your mortgage repayments, lenders will not immediately seek to take possession of your property.

Under the Mortgage Conduct of Business[2] rules set by the Financial Conduct Authority, a mortgage lender must make reasonable efforts to make arrangements with the borrower to pay the money that is owed ('arrears'). However, this does underline the importance of having your finances in order before deciding to purchase a property.

The amount you need to borrow depends on the purchase price of your property and the size of your deposit. Some lenders offer small deposit mortgages where you only need 5% of the purchase price for the deposit; i.e. if your property is £200,000, the deposit is £10,000. However, a 5% deposit is by no way the norm.

Expert's View

Many High-Street lenders and smaller building societies are happy to lend with only a 5% deposit on second-hand properties. Generally, the more deposit you contribute, the lower the interest rate. Typically, a 10% deposit will offer a considerably lower interest rate than a 5% deposit mortgage Although the deposit can be any amount, typical increments are 5% / 10% / 15% / 25% / 40%. There is the odd lender who will offer a mortgage with a 20% or even 50% deposits from the borrower.

Mathew Kind,
Financial Services Director

The deposit size will also be affected by the planned purpose of the property. The deposits listed above are for mortgages for a main residence. If a person already owns a residence and is taking out a mortgage to purchase another property for buy-to-let, the lender might require a higher level of deposit, as there is more uncertainty associated with the transactions (i.e. finding tenants, repaying a second mortgage).

What you do for work is important for the lender, as it is an indication of what monthly repayment you will be able to make. The type of your employment, your income, how long you have been with your employer, whether you are self-employed: all of these are taken into consideration. For example, if you are self-employed, lenders will hesitate at approving your application if you have been self-employed for less than 2 years.

When applying for a mortgage, it is always good to get the following prepared for the mortgage advisor to speed up the process:

a)   Identification documents;
b)   Bank statements for the last 3 months;
c)   Payslips (or business accounts if self-employed) for the last 3 months; and
d)   A credit file sourced from Experian/Equifax/Noddle.

A credit file is essentially a report containing information about your past financial behaviour. It may include: times when you have borrowed money, whether you are on the electoral register, if you have been late on your repayments or repaid on time and in full, whether you have ever been declared bankrupt before, how much you currently owe etcetera.

Under the Consumer Credit Act 1974, the providers mentioned above must provide you with your credit report for no more than £2, which you can access online or by requesting a paper copy.

It is important to note that lenders do not necessarily use the same criteria provided in a credit report. One might care more about how often you borrow money, while another might care more about the number of times you have been late on repayments. However, a credit file gives you a general idea of what your chances are of having your mortgage approved.

You will find that many mortgages will refuse to lend to buyers who do not have at least 2, often 3 years of continuous address history in the UK. This is something to bear in mind if you have recently moved from overseas.

b. GOVERNMENT SPONSORED LOANS

The government has a Help to Buy Equity Loan scheme that is providing a special class of loans for purchases that meet the following conditions:

» The property is a new-build property;
» Its value is up to £600,000; and
» The property will be used as the residence of the borrower (i.e. the property cannot be buy-to-let) and must be the onlyresidence of the borrower (i.e. you are not eligible if purchasing a second home).

If all of the above conditions are met, the buyer needs to contribute a 5% deposit towards the purchase. The government will lend the buyer up to 20% of the value if the property is outside of London. If the property is in London, the government will lend the buyer up to 40% of the value of the property. It is the responsibility of the buyer to find a mortgage for the difference.

For example, if you are buying a property in London for £500,000, then you need to contribute a £25,000 deposit (5% of the total price). Then the government can lend you £200,000 (40% of the total price), in which case you will have to find a mortgage for the remaining £275,000 (55% of the total price).

The government loan is interest free for the first 5 years. In the 6th year, you are charged a 1.75% interest on the loan's value. The interest then increases based on the Retail Price Index plus 1%. The loan must be repaid after 25 years or when you sell your home, whichever comes first. More information about the scheme can be found on the Affordable Home Ownership web-site[3].

c.   MORTGAGE BROKERS

It is not absolutely necessary to go through a mortgage broker in order to find a mortgage. However, in exchange for a fee, most mortgage brokers offer comprehensive mortgage searches, which provide access to a large variety of offers from multiple lenders, as well as potentially preferential rates and deals that you would not normally find by going straight to a bank.

Mortgage brokers also provide someone to work with you through the process, making sure you get individually tailored advice regarding your mortgage, as well as concerning conveyancing issues and home insurance.

The process of getting a mortgage can take over one month dependant on how many people are involved in the property-chain. A mortgage broker may help to streamline the process; however, you should bear in mind that their services will come at a fee. The prices will obviously differ based on the broker, the amount borrowed and the location.

These advisors are working in your interests rather than those of the lender. They not only recommend a mortgage that is suitable to your circumstances, they also explain the cost and risk of the proposed mortgage.

When first contacting a mortgage broker, you will be asked to provide:

a)   The purchase price of the property;

b)   The amount you can provide for your deposit;

c)   The level of property you are looking at; and

d)   What your occupation is and your monthly salary.

Thus, it will speed up the process if you have that information ready before approaching a mortgage broker. Additionally, it may be helpful to send information about your monthly outgoings, such as: groceries, clothing, utility bills, council tax, and travel expenses etcetera.

d.   MORTGAGE DEFAULT

Not repaying your mortgage can have serious consequences. The details of the process will be recorded in the mortgage documents and will list the different events that would constitute default. Usually, one of the following three conditions will have to be present, for the lender to trigger the process of taking possession of the property: the lender had served a notice on the borrower requiring repayment of the loan and the borrower failed to comply with it for 3 months; the interest due on the mortgage is 3 months in arrears; the borrower has breached a term of the mortgage deed.

Those events will give the lender the right to take possession of the property and sell it. Alternatively, if tenants currently occupy the property, the lender might be satisfied with intercepting the income from the tenants.

The lenders must follow the Mortgage Conduct of Business Rules[4] created by the Financial Conduct Authority. Those rules are aimed at providing some degree of protection to borrowers, by stipulating that lenders must treat borrowers fairly and give them reasonable chances to repay any arrears. As a result, the borrower will usually start a process of negotiations with the lender to come up with a suitable arrangement for repaying any arrears.

If no such negotiations take place, or if they are unsuccessful, the lender can start a possession action, the ultimate point of which is to take possession of the property. Even at this stage, the borrower can prevent this by agreeing to a reasonable repayment schedule. Such a schedule can be negotiated directly with the lender or as a part of the court proceedings. The court will usually try to find the most reasonable and amicable solution to the problem. However, if the borrower is not adhering to the repayment schedule agreed with the lender or ordered by the court, then the lender will successfully take possession of the property.

Once the lender has possession, it can sell the property. However, the lender does have a duty to the borrower to act in good faith and take reasonable care to obtain the market value for the property. However, this does not include delaying the sale of the property to obtain a better market price.

There are a number of rules specifying how the proceeds of the sale should be applied. The lender must apply the proceeds to redeem any prior mortgages – mortgages granted before the one owned by the lender who is taking possession and selling the property. The lender will use the remaining proceeds to recover its expenses in selling the property. Then the lender will use the remainder to redeem its own mortgage. Following that, the lender will discharge any remaining mortgages. Finally, the remainder of the sale proceeds will be advanced to the borrower.

This is the legal process of using the proceeds of sale of a property in default on a mortgage. However, some of those steps will not be relevant for most mortgages. Typically, a property is subject to a single mortgage, and as a result the lender will simply use the proceeds to cover its cost of sale and the balance on its own mortgage. The remaining proceeds will be advanced to the borrower.

It is important to note that defaulting on your mortgage will have a lasting impact on your credit score and will severely impact your chances of receiving mortgage lending in the future.

e.   THE LENDING PROCESS

The lending process will consist of several meetings with the lenders to go over the requirements of each party to the transaction. The process will start with a mortgage application made to the lender. The application will have to be supported by a number of documents confirming the identity of the borrower and their income. The lender will process the application to identify any irregularities and confirm any missing information. If the applications meet the requirements, the lender will order a valuation of the property the borrower is planning to purchase. Once the lender has the valuation, it will approve or reject the application. Information detailing the decision of the lender will be sent to both the applicant and his legal representative. If the application was successful, the lender will provide the mortgage offer that is listing the lending conditions. It is very important for borrowers to examine the offer and ensure that it satisfies their financial needs. It is still possible to negotiate changes to the offer at this stage – for example if your parents offered to help you with the deposit and now you require a smaller loan.

Expert's View

The lending process will usually start with an initial meeting to qualify the client. This would typically include an agreement in principle to establish affordability/lending capacity and perform a credit check. In order to do this, the lender would conduct a full 'fact find' with a qualified mortgage advisor, who will obtain all the relevant levels of information required and collate the relevant documentation. This would include the important checks of identify, employment and income, and possibly existing mortgage statements, bills, or even evidence of shopping expenditure.

The first meeting will be followed by a discussion to advise the client on the best-case scenario available to him, to go over regulation, how lenders operate under the Financial Conduct Authority and what they are required to do for their clients, as well as the process of buying a house or re-mortgaging.

It is at this stage that the lender would present you, the client, with some indicative fees for mortgage costs and costs associated with the lending process. Usually, a subsequent meeting will then be arranged once a property has been found to finalise the borrowing scenario and formalise any advice given.

After the agreements are signed the adviser will process the application. At this stage, some advisers will discuss protection, such as Payment Protection Insurance (which may enable borrowers to ensure repayment of credit if they were to pass away, becomes ill or disabled, lose their job, or faces other circumstances that may prevent them from meeting the repayments), or arrange another meeting to go through the various protection schemes that they offer. A re-mortgage may not require this whole process and may even be done in one sitting, dependent on the complexity of research required.

Mathew Kind,
Financial Services Director

Once the offer is signed, the borrower has committed to the conditions listed in it. However, the release of the funds is still conditional on the satisfaction of numerous conditions. The lender will require substantial amounts of information about the property – from the legal title, to an environmental search, to insurance information. Once all the information that is requested by the lender has been provided, the lender will be able to release the funds to the borrower's legal representative. We will discuss the process of obtaining the needed property information and communicating it to the lender throughout the following chapters.

f.   FAMILY AND FRIENDS

The English Housing Survey[5] indicates that in 2015 about 27% of first-time property buyers relied on friends and family for the purchase of their property. Usually, this involves receiving assistance from your parents for the deposit required for the purchase. Reliance on family financing is so widespread that some agencies rank parents as the 10th largest mortgage lender in the UK, providing the deposits for almost 300,000 mortgages.

Whether the money is gift or a loan will be the choice of the parents and can have tax implications for them. However, parents might want to take certain precautions when funding the purchase for a young couple, to ensure that if the couple splits, the money is not divided between them.

2.   LOCATING YOUR PROPERTY OR FINDING A BUYER

Once you have set your budget and know if a mortgage is available to you, the next step is to begin looking around for your property. For most people, the number of bedrooms and square footage will be the most important factors to consider. Interestingly, the number of the rooms usually has a higher impact on the price of a property than the actual size of the rooms.

Another important element is the condition of the property. Recent renovations can affect the comfort and the aesthetics of a property, as well as the monthly utility bills. Consider whether the windows of the property are double-glazed or if the property has had loft and wall insulation done. A properly insulated property can save you hundreds in energy bills; the Energy Performance Certificate[6] (EPC) should give you a good indication of the energy efficiency of the property.

Alternatively, you might prioritise the location of the property: whether the property is placed next to a noisy road, if it is in walking distance from public transport, if shops and schools are nearby or whether crime rates in the area are low.

All of these are relevant considerations for both the future homeowner and for the buy-to-let investor, because these are things that tenants bear in mind when deciding where they would like to live.

Given that there are so many factors to bear in mind, it may be worthwhile to find an estate agent to help you with this process. Estate agents combine professional marketing skill, years of industry experience and a vast network of contacts to provide sellers with a competitive advantage.

Expert's View

My first move would be to meet the seller to discuss their hopes and aspirations. A service would then be tailored to their requirements. I would then prepare a detailed valuation and marketing strategy. If the client favored me with his/her instructions, I would then prepare marketing particulars, prepare floor plans, and take photos. A database of prospective buyers would be contacted at the same time as placing the property on the market. As a minimum, the property would be placed on all popular Internet sites and some properties would benefit from additional marketing (e.g. magazines). A board would be ordered where appropriate.

Andrew Kay,
Commercial and Residential Property Expert

a. ESTATE AGENTS

A seller of a property will have the option of using estate agents. Of course, the services of an estate agent come at a cost. Different arrangements exist, depending on the local property market and the specific needs of the seller. However, most agents offer a few typical cost arrangements.

Expert's View

Sole Agency: This is where only one agent can market the property and introduce a buyer; they will have an exclusive term. Fees will normally range from 1% plus vat to 3% plus vat. A sole agent's interests are completely aligned with the seller's interests.

Joint Sole Agency: This is where two agents can offer the property for sale, it is generally accepted that the agent who sells the property will receive the full commission but some agencies may choose to split the commission. This option will normally be 0.5% more expensive than a sole agency commission.

Multiple Agency: This is where more than two estate agents can offer the property for sale. This is the most expensive option and will normally be 1% more expensive than a sole agency commission. Some buyers may feel that there is a problem with a property listed with lots of estate agents and that the seller is desperate to sell. It is better to choose a sole agent with a good track record who will focus on finding the best buyer for the property, rather than rush to find an unsuitable buyer just to beat the competition.

Robert Wright,
Real Estate Specialist

Their extensive experience in marketing properties makes estate agents the best guide for providing correct property valuation. As discussed above, many different factors impact the value of a property, from size and location, to condition and styling.

Expert's View

It is not uncommon for buyers and sellers to negotiate without the assistance of an estate agent. However, in most cases the people involved are not experts in valuation. I, for example, have over 30 years of experience in the Birmingham property market - 15 as a solicitor and 16 as an estate agent. With the services of an expert, the party can be sure they are not underselling or overpaying. Also, they will be fully aware of the negatives and positives concerning the property in particular: the immediate vicinity, the potential outgoings and the future for the area, etcetera. Additional benefits are that a good, honest agent will only have their clients' best interests at heart. The negotiations will be more reasonable, less emotional, more factual and advice on all situations will produce the best outcome. An agent will also be able to act as a middle man in the legal process - as a former solicitor, I often suggest solutions for problems which would otherwise jeopardise a transaction and cost both parties considerable sums in wasted costs.

Andrew Kay,
Commercial and Residential Property Expert

Estate agents are the preferred option for first-time sellers that do not know the local market well. And while their services come at a cost, it is important to appreciate the value a good agent can bring to the transaction. Of course, this raises an important question – What is a good estate agent? How do we decide whom to entrust with the sale of our home? There are many factors to consider when choosing an agent, from the prices they charge, to the marketing approach they use, to the positioning they have in the local market.

Expert's View

The most common mistake is choosing the cheapest agent. The cheapest agent is unlikely to be able to afford the best marketing and the best staff to sell the property for the best price and the cheapest agent never has the largest market share. A recent example illustrates the dangers of choosing the cheapest agent. The starkest case was a flat that went to the market with a cheaper agent at £400,000. A few days later we marketed a very similar flat a few doors away for £425,000. We found a buyer within a few days at £20,000 above the asking price (£445,000). The other client was still on the market 3 months later and eventually sold at £380,000. The difference in fee was approximately £3000 plus vat but it cost the client £65,000, lost time, having to be inconvenienced by viewings for months on end and they lost the property they wanted to buy due to the amount of time it took them to find a buyer. Instruct the best agent not the cheapest.

Robert Wright,
Real Estate Specialist

b. INDEPENDENT WORK

If you feel confident in your skills and approach, you can try to market the property yourself. However, there are a number of techniques to keep in mind, in order to reach a successful outcome.

Doing extensive research of the neighbouring properties and coming up with a reasonable value for your own property is absolutely crucial. Starting with a very high initial valuation often means that the property goes unsold for a long period of time. This has a bad effect on the property, as it will be seen as undesirable. Buyers are more interested in "fresh" properties that were listed recently and will be very suspicious of an old offer. Thus, starting with a reasonable price is important and can often lead to significant interest and a "bidding war" for your property. Often, the final sell price can increase noticeably after you have asked all interested parties to submit their best and final offers.

Buyers are also advised to approach the property with a reasonable offer. Submitting a very low initial offer does not present you as a serious contender. It is important to make the seller feel confident about your intentions. Also, it is important to anticipate the offers of the other buyers. It might be a good idea to stay away from round numbers – considering another buyer's final offer is likely £500,000, it is advisable to have a final offer of £502,000. You would be paying an additional £2,000 however you would not lose a property you really like and avoid incurring the additional expense of starting the search process from the beginning again.

3. SURVEYS AND VALUATIONS

After you have chosen a property that fits your requirements and have secured the finances to purchase it, it is important to learn more about the property.

A valuation report will state what the value of the property is; however this will not specify the condition of the property. It will take into account a large number of factors including location of the property, its size, and its condition etcetera. The lender needs to know the value of the property in order to approve the mortgage for the property. As a part of reviewing the mortgage application, the bank will instruct a Royal Institute of Chartered Surveyors[7] (RICS) registered valuer to perform a valuation for secured lending purposes. When applying for a mortgage, it is advisable to ask the lender who will cover the cost of the valuation report and whether you can review the valuation report. While the lender will order a valuation report, the property buyer can also order such a report and include it in the mortgage application to facilitate the process. Sometimes valuation reports are not connected with a property purchase, they are instead done for the re-mortgage of an existing home.

A RICS[7] Homebuyers Report also includes a valuation of the property and a rebuild cost. However, this report also includes advice on necessary repairs and maintenance issues. The report will indicate whether any elements of the property do not meet the current building regulations. This report is a valuation report with some elements of a building survey. However, this report is a surface examination – for example the surveyor will not examine behind the furniture.

Surveys are more extensive reports on the building; as such they will usually come at a higher cost. For this reason, they are often commissioned after an offer has been made, during the pre-exchange enquires. We will discuss these in more detail in Chapter 3.

4. INSURANCE

Buying insurance is an important element of home ownership. Very often homeowners are not left with a free choice of whether to purchase insurance. Banks and Building Societies can require you to purchase insurance, just like they can require a building survey on the property. The aim of the lenders is to protect the property that is subject to the mortgage. There are usually two kinds of insurance to consider:

»   a building insurance, that will cover the destruction of a property (e.g. fire) and will be based on its reconstruction value. Lenders will require this type of insurance.

» a contents insurance, that will cover elements within the property (e.g. TVs, kitchen equipment, etcetera).

It is important to note that the insurance coverage should start from the time of contract exchange, in order to minimize risk for the buyer. Determining who is responsible for the property, in case it suffers any damage between the exchange of contracts and the completion of the sale, will involve a complicated and costly legal process. Also, the buyer should consider using the services of an insurance broker, as this will facilitate the process of obtaining insurance tailored to the buyer's specific needs.

Expert's View

A buyer should arrange cover on their properties upon exchange of contracts. They are committed to purchasing the property at that point so it is prudent to ensure the property is covered properly, by an appropriate policy, up to completion. The seller is responsible for maintaining insurance but the buyer has no guarantee the seller will. If you suffered losses following a fire but the seller had cancelled the insurance, the resulting legal implications could quickly turn into a nightmare. So, it is important that the buyer protects his investment by buying insurance coverage from the time of exchange.

Brokers will provide advice that is impartial and suited to your needs. Insurance companies sell their own products, so you may not be offered what is most appropriate for your needs. Also, the policyholder is left to deal with the insurance company in the event of a claim, whereas a part of a broker's job is to ensure that the claim is settled on

the best possible terms, as quickly as possible.
Daniel Innes,
Insurance Managing Director

While insurance policies are very specific to the providers that offer them, there is generally a type of coverage aimed at rental properties. This type of insurance will provide protection in the case of damage to the building, loss of rental income, legal liability arising from misuse by the tenants, etcetera.

Expert's View

Ordinary home insurance does not meet the needs for rental properties, which is why landlords are advised to get specialist cover.

Most buy to let policies now include key covers to fully protect landlords including:

» *Property Owners/Landlord's Liability - This kind of insurance will cover accidental injuries incurred by your tenants or other third parties in the property e.g. if they suffer any injuries from a bad fall down the stairs that is proven to be your liability.*

» *Legal expenses cover: this can cover your costs if you are involved in a legal dispute with your tenant potentially including tenancy disputes (if the right insurer is chosen)*

» *Some other insurers can also cover rent guarantee or home emergency cover but you should carefully check the extent of cover and terms attached to these.*

Daniel Innes,
Insurance Managing Director

Once you have determined your preferred property and acquired a loan, it is strongly advised that you seek out the services of a legal professional experienced in residential conveyancing. There is a large number of legal considerations to bear in mind when purchasing/selling property.

However, there are also a great number of ways to ensure that the conveyancing process is as quick as possible and that costs are kept to a minimum. The following chapters will walk a prospective buyer or seller through this process, highlighting the stages at which a buyer or seller can lessen the strain on their mind and wallet.

CHAPTER TWO

Preparing to Purchase or Sell your Property

Now we begin to explore the legal aspects of buying or selling a property. The next stage is to instruct a conveyance/solicitor. If you are selling, you will normally go to see a conveyancer or solicitor at the point where you have accepted an offer from a buyer. If you are buying, you will normally go to see a conveyancer/solicitor when you have located your intended property, had your offer accepted and have a mortgage agreement in place.

In the UK, a property could have several different types of legal titles. The difference will have an impact on different parts of the conveyancing process: from the documents used to the permission needed.

1. TYPES OF LEGAL TITLE

The legal title of the property you are considering to purchase will have an impact on the instructions you must give to your legal representative and on the type of due diligence that they must perform. In England and Wales, your ownership in land can take two forms: Freehold or Leasehold. It is important to explain the differences between Freehold and Leasehold interests in order to fully understand the rights and obligations associated with your purchase.

a. FREEHOLDS & LEASEHOLDS

If you own the freehold, you own it outright: both the outlined land and the property built on it. Your ownership is unconditional and is not subject to any time constraints. Thus, a freeholder could own the land until their death, at which point it will pass according to the person's Will. If the person has not made a Will, then the land will pass according to the rules of intestacy, through the process of administration of the estate.

However, if you own the leasehold, you merely own the property for the duration of the lease agreement with the freeholder, usually for periodic payment. In short, your ownership will end once the time on your lease runs out and, unless you manage to extend the lease, ownership will return to the freeholder.

Many leases are created from earlier leases, called 'superior leases', with all leases traced back to the freehold. Leasehold lengths vary widely, however you can generally expect them to be between 999 years and 99 years.

Between the two, it is fair to say that owning the freehold is generally more desirable. If you have a freehold, you can live at ease in the knowledge that your ownership is firmly set in stone, while a leaseholder will have the cloud of an expiration date hanging over their head. Unlike a leaseholder, a freeholder will not need to pay annual ground rent.

Ground rent is usually included in leasehold properties. While you have paid a lump sum for the purchase of the leasehold (i.e. £500,000 paid for a 125-year lease of the property), it is likely that you will also have to make an annual ground rent payment. The amount you will have to pay differs greatly between properties, with owners of new-build flats charging as high as a few hundred pounds per year, and owners of ex-local authority flats requiring as low as only £20 per year. It is not uncommon for ground rent to be escalating – for example it might start at £50 for the first ten years, and then increase by £10 for each additional ten years of the lease. All the formal requirements regarding the ground rent will be stipulated in the lease agreement.

If you were a leaseholder, the ground rent you pay will go straight into the pockets of the freeholder, which will leave you with no rights over the property after the end of the lease. As a freeholder, the responsibility in maintaining the property (i.e. the floors, the walls, the roof etcetera) is yours, however leaseholders will frequently have to pay maintenance fees, service charges and perhaps a proportion of the buildings insurance. Service charges are expenses associated with the cost of maintaining the common spaces in an apartment building.

It is important to note that the years left on the lease will have an impact on a buyer's ability to obtain a mortgage.

Expert's View

Different lenders have different approaches to establishing if a leasehold property qualifies for mortgage lending, based on its term. One approach is to examine the number of years left on the lease. Only a few lenders will consider a lease with only 40 years remaining at the time of application. Typically, lenders will require a lease with at least 70-80 years remaining, in order to provide financing.

Another approach is to demand a specific number of years after the repayment of the mortgage. If the mortgage term is 30 years and the lender requires 25 additional years, then the leasehold will have to be for a minimum of 55 years. Some lenders might combine the two approaches,

requiring, for example, 60 years left of the lease,
with at least 35 years left after the end of the
mortgage.

Mathew Kind,
Financial Services Director

Lenders are increasingly looking for longer lease terms as part of their lending criteria, with some lenders wanting the unexpired lease term to be as long as 95 years. A lease term close to 80 years may be purchased with a mortgage replace with, however, cost consideration of extending the lease would need to be factored in as the risk is that no mortgage funding will be available to a buyer when you will look to sell your property further down the line.

b.   A SHARE OF THE FREEHOLD AND THE COMMONHOLD

Alternatively, you may come across a seller who owns the leasehold as well as a share of the freehold. This is where a number of leaseholders have bought the freehold together. The benefit of doing this is that you gain more control over the property (rights to renovate, maintain, etcetera.). Furthermore, having a share of the freehold will make it easier for you, the leaseholder for example, to extend your lease once the terms comes to an end.

Commonholds were introduced with the Commonhold and Leasehold Reform Act 2002[8] and the concept only applies to multi-occupancy buildings (e.g. a block of flats). Each flat becomes a freehold unit so each owner becomes the freeholder of their flat. The common areas (e.g. stairways, common rooms) are owned and managed by a Commonhold Association. However, commonholds are rarely found on the property market.

c.   NEW-BUILD PROPERTIES

It is common for building companies to sell properties that are in

24

the process of construction, or that have not even been commenced. Buying such new developments is a relatively recent trend. Usually, people would like to see the actual property before purchasing it. With new developments, you are usually limited to examining the development plans and sketches, and some multi-media content like presentations and virtual 3D renditions of the property. This might not give a complete picture of your new home. The plans of the property are often subject to some changes. Many contracts for new developments stipulate that the building company can deviate from the initial plans by a certain percentage (usually 5%), if the building process requires it. As a result, the kitchen set you pre-ordered for your new property might very well not fit in the kitchen anymore.

The layout and ambiance of the home are not the only concerns a buyer should have when it comes to new developments. The conveyancing process should involve a detailed analysis of the building company and of the financing needed for the acquisition.

Expert's View

The usual due diligence process does not take into account some fundamental risks that might arise with new developments. One such risk is developer insolvency: a company might start building and then become insolvent. Also, the company might not be able to obtain the additional financing needed to complete the development.

A buyer should consider their own financial position too- if you are exchanging contracts today for a development that will be completed in, let us say, 3 years, you are unlikely to be able to obtain mortgage funding at the point of exchange of contracts. Lenders are more likely to consider lending on a new build property usually no more than 3 months before the completion of the property. So, you run the risk a lender may not lend at all or may not lend in time when you apply for a mortgage before completion of the new build property. This may be due to a change in your personal financial circumstances or there may be a limited number of lenders willing to lend on new build properties at the time you apply for a mortgage. It sensible to ensure you have a contingency in place to fund the purchase you are unable to secure a mortgage.

Market valuation is also an important factor. You could pay £1 million for something on the date of exchange of contracts, hoping the price will increase by the time you complete. However, there is always a possibility that the price of the property goes down. In the worst-case scenario, you may have a negative equity situation whereby you will have to deposit more money than budgeted for to be able to complete the purchase.

Philip Li,
Solicitor-Partner

There are certain steps that can be taken to minimize the risk of buying a new development. For example, certain types of insurance cover the deposit you pay to the developer. As a result, if there are any complications and the building company cannot finish the development, your deposit is insured and you will receive compensation. This is just one example of the specific nature of new developments. You are advised to discuss such an investment with your legal representative in detail.

2. CHOOSING YOUR CONVEYANCER/SOLICITOR

It may be helpful to explain the difference between conveyancers and solicitors. Both are legal professionals, however solicitors are qualified practitioners with training in various areas of law, whereas licenced conveyancers are specialised in property.

The services of licenced conveyancers are generally more affordable than those of solicitors, however cost should not be your only concern. As the conveyancing process entails a hefty amount of paperwork, you want a practitioner who will keep to deadlines and be meticulous in checking all the boxes. Moreover, you want a practitioner with whom you can maintain a stable line of communication, so that you can track their progress and contact if you have any questions.

The above qualities are crucial because delays can add costs and, in the worst-case scenario, cause a purchase/sale to fall through. Generally, a licenced conveyancer will be sufficient to deal with the purchase or sale of your property, however you might consider going to a solicitor if your case seems more complex: e.g. a property you want to buy or sell has been subject to an on-going dispute relating to boundary issues.

If your estate agent recommends a licenced conveyancer/solicitor for your purchase/sale, a good idea would be to ask if they receive commission for the recommendation. Where this is the case, using the estate agent's recommendation could add to your expenses, as the recommended practitioner's fees may include the agent's commission.

If you need a mortgage for your purchase, another important point is that lenders will often want you to use a licenced conveyancer/solicitor that is on their panel. Should the legal representative you have instructed not be on the lender's panel, your lender will normally instruct their own legal representatives (separate from your legal representatives) from their panel to act on their behalf and require you to pay the costs for their legal work. For example, at the time of writing of this book, HSBC charges you £295[9] for this service.

We will be referring to both solicitors and licensed conveyancers as "legal representatives" throughout the rest of this chapter.

3. THE ROLE OF THE LEGAL REPRESENTATIVE

The legal representative that both sides employ will navigate the property transaction. Usually, a residential property transaction will take about 8 weeks from start to finish. This depends largely on the different searches that a legal representative has to undertake. Generally, those involve inspecting the legal title of the property, whether it is subject to a mortgage, what restrictions and obligations are attached to it, what utilities are available, what repairs might be needed, etcetera.

The guiding principle of property transactions is caveat emptor – this basically means that the buyer is responsible for inspecting the quality of the property. For the purpose, the buyer's legal representative raises requisitions about any potential problems and the seller's legal representative responds to them. This process of raising inquiries is called 'due diligence'.

Expert's View

I think that the most important part of a property transaction is the legal due diligence process, which takes place before the exchange of contracts. Essentially, it's an exercise of gathering as much information about the property as possible from both the seller's solicitors and own enquires and searches. This includes information from the title register, results of the property searches, and from the seller himself.

There are standard enquiries which the sellers

will answer for example, whether there have been any disputes with the use and enjoyment of the property, what utilities the property benefits from, whether any alterations or building works have been carried out to the property which may have required planning permission or building regulations consent We gather this information, review it and summarise the important and relevant points for the client to enable the client to make a considered decision as to whether or not to proceed with the purchase.

Philip Li,

Solicitor-Partner

Your requests in relation to any legal work are known as 'instructions'. Once you instruct a legal representative, they will normally send you a retainer letter confirming your instructions. The work they undertake on your behalf will follow from these instructions and from their 'terms of engagement', which will set out what you have authorised them to do on your behalf, as well as their charges.

Usually, the estate agent or the buyer and seller will know who the legal representative of the other party is and they will communicate that information to their legal representative. At this stage, the legal representatives will contact each other and communicate that they have been instructed to act on the transaction. Then they will proceed with exchanging information about the property. The nature of the information they will communicate is the subject of the subsequent chapters.

4. ANTI-MONEY LAUNDERING (AML) CHECKS

It is important to bear in mind that your legal representative will not be able to immediately take your instructions and start working on the transaction. As professionals involved with high-value transactions, they are required by the Money Laundering Regulations 2007 to perform Anti Money Laundering (AML) checks on all their clients before proceeding with any of their client-specific work.

AML checks exist in order to prevent the services of legal representatives from being used to transfer the proceeds of crime or to finance terrorism. We will go over these checks in more detail further on; you are, after all, more concerned about buying or selling your property. However, you will be interested to know what you need to bring, so your legal representative can complete these checks promptly and begin taking instructions from you.

Your legal representative is required to identify you i.e. ask your name and address, and then verify your identity via some evidence that supports your claim. It's become even more crucial to do this given the rise in the number of cases involving identity fraud in property transactions. There is a host of original documents that can be used for verification purposes, although most individuals can and will provide some of the following:

1. Proofs of ID:
    a) A current signed passport;
    b) A current driver's licence;
    c) A current EEA member state identity card.
2. Proofs of address:
    a) A council tax bill;
    b) A utility bill or statement;
    c) A bank, building society or credit union statement or passbook containing current address.

Identity checks are more complicated when the transaction involves international parties, whether individuals or companies. For example, if the buyer is a foreign citizen, the legal representative must check if the passport presented is registered. The services of a search agent, conducting AML checks, might be employed at this stage.

Furthermore, if a foreign national presents any documents executed in a foreign jurisdiction – i.e. a statutory declaration executed by a foreign solicitor – those documents will have to be notarized and translated in order to have effect in the United Kingdom.

As can be seen, the majority of these original documents must be current, i.e. presently valid. Similarly, the council tax bill, utility bill (electricity, gas, water etcetera.) or bank statement that you provide must have been issued within three months of the date when you present it to your legal representative. Most firms will require two types of ID so be sure to bring at least two.

The list of acceptable documents here is not exhaustive. Also, there are alternative documents for persons who are not UK residents and for persons who cannot provide standard documents for verification. If curious, please check the Law Society's[10] website for further guidance.

Once you provide your legal representative with these documents, they will normally check them by using an electronic verification service provider, who crosschecks your details with other independent sources. At the time of writing of this book, providers of AML checks usually charge between £5 and £20 for conducting the checks.

5.   THE SELLER'S PACK

If you are selling a property, it is probably a good idea to have decided on which legal representative you are going to use around the point you engaged an estate agent. By doing so, you will likely reduce the possibility of delays and place yourself in a position to begin the conveyancing process as soon as possible once you have accepted a buyer's offer.

Having passed the AML checks, your meeting with the legal representative will mainly be about providing information about the property you intend to sell. Thus, your legal representative should provide you with a number of questionnaires to complete, which will detail important pieces of information that should be disclosed to the buyer's legal representative.

The documents that your legal representative will seek to obtain once they begin to take instructions from you will depend on whether you are purchasing freehold or leasehold property. Some of the forms listed below are relevant for only one of the two main types of property and others are relevant for both types:

i)   Official Copy of the Title Register;
ii)   TA6: Property Information Form;
iii) TA7 or TA9: Leasehold Information Form & Commonhold Information Form;
iv)   TA10: Fittings and Contents Form;
v)   TA13: Completion Information and Undertakings;
vi)   Draft Contract;
vii) LPE1;
viii) License to Assign.

We will provide some basic information about each type of form below, which may be useful for following the progress of the transaction. We have also included explanations of the content and nature of some of the forms that your legal representative might require you to complete.

i)   Official Copy of the Title Register

In order to prove ownership of a registered property, the seller must obtain official copies of the title (which will contain the names of the owners of the property and associated land).

The majority of land in England and Wales is registered. Your legal representative will order an official copy of your property's title register together with the title plan from the Land Registry, which should show that you own the land and the form of your legal ownership. Usually legal representatives have access to the Land Registry Business e-services, which should enable them to download an official copy of the Title Registry and title plan instantaneously.

If you are curious, you can purchase an online unofficial copy through the Land Registry's[11] website. At the time of writing of this book, the cost of purchasing an online unofficial copy of the title registry is £3 and the cost of ordering an unofficial plan is also £3.

If you would like to order an official copy of the title registry yourself, the cost would be £7 and this would have to be done by filling out form OC1[12] and sending this through the mail to the Land Registry together with a £7 fee for the Official copy and a further £7 for the title plan.

It is worth noting that although electronic copies of the Official Copy of the Title Register and Title Plan are not available to those unable to register on the Land Registry's Business e-services, they can be bought through third party websites, such as iCompile Searches, at a higher price. You will need to refer to the third party's price guide.

ii) TA6: Property Information Form

Whatever the type of property you are selling might be (i.e. freehold, leasehold) this will be the first document you should fill out. The TA6 is not an absolute requirement; however failing to provide the information required by it can cause delays. A sample TA6[13] form can be found on the website of the Law Society.

As the form will state, you are not expected to have any legal or technical knowledge, so simply try to give answers to the best of your knowledge. If you feel confused by any of the terms or concepts, you should ask your legal representative to explain them, and ensure you do not give answers to questions you do not know. Rather, you should inform your legal representative that you do not know. It is crucial that you provide information that is complete or correct to the best of your knowledge, as doing otherwise could cause the buyer to stall the sale or even claim compensation from you.

The TA6 covers an extensive range of issues that can relate to the seller's property and will most likely be the object of the buyer's concern. These include:

» **Boundaries:**

Among other things, these questions mainly relate to whose responsibility it is to maintain boundaries or boundary features (e.g. hedges, fences, walls, etcetera).

Facts relating to boundaries are important because they are often the source of on-going or future disputes between neighbours or local authorities, with potential financial repercussions. For instance, you may unknowingly be required to maintain a boundary feature.

» **Disputes and Complaints:**

These questions relate to whether there are any existing disputes/complaints, details of such disputes/complaints, and whether anything might lead to a future dispute/complaint.

» **Notices and Proposals:**

These questions relate to letters or communications, from neighbours, local authorities or governmental departments, which could potentially affect the property in question.

» **Alterations, Planning and Building Control:**

These questions relate to whether alterations or changes have been made to the property and if such works have been properly approved. For example, the owner could have built a conservatory, an extension, or had solar panels installed.

If such alterations have been made and the owner did not obtain permission or approval, then the owner may be served with an enforcement notice to return things to the way they were before.

» **Guarantees and Warranties:**

These questions primarily concern works that may have been

done on the property: whether the associated guarantees/warranties can be transferred to the buyer and whether claims have already been made in relation to such guarantees/warranties.

» **Insurance:**

These questions relate to whether the seller already has insurance taken out on the property, whether they have made any past or present claims and, if it has an existing insurance policy, whether the property has been subject to high excesses or premiums, or unusual conditions.

» **Environment Matters:**

These questions relate to a wide range of environmental risks. The most relevant ones are: whether the property is in a flood-risk area and whether the property might be affected by radon. It is fairly self-explanatory why you would want to know if the property was in a flood-risk area, however radon is a less well-known phenomena.

Radon is a naturally occurring inert gas, which is found in all rocks and soil. Furthermore, it can enter properties from the ground. Most importantly, it produces a radioactive dust in the air we breathe, which increases your risk of lung cancer.

If you feel concerned about a property being in a radon-risk area, you may want to check with your legal representatives if you should order a radon address search online via UKradon[14].

The form also asks for a copy of the Energy Performance Certificate[6] of the property. This certificate gives a property an energy fficiency rating from A (most efficient) to G (least efficient) and makes recommendations about making the property more energy efficient. Providing such a certificate is mandatory upon building, selling or renting a property in the UK. The certificate is prepared by an accredited assessor and is valid for 10 years. However, if there are any material changes to the property (i.e. new boiler system or new window insulation installed), a new certificate needs to be obtained. Recent legislative changes stipulate that from 1st April 2018 it will not be possible to rent out a property that has a rating lower than E (i.e. ratings of F or G), unless certain exemptions apply.

» **Rights and Informal Arrangements:**
These questions cover a broad range of topics, such as: whether any leases under 7 years exist or if the land has certain rights or liability attached to it (i.e. rights to mines and minerals, manorial rights, chancel repair).

» **Parking:**
Those questions ask for the description of the parking arrangements and for whether there are any licenses that need to be obtained. The presence of a Controlled Parking Zone should be indicated as well – this is an area where there are restrictions on parking at certain times. Furthermore, there should be details about a local authority-parking scheme operated by the council, if such a scheme exists.

» **Other Charges:**
This section asks for the presence of additional charges affecting the property. One example is a charge to a management company. The seller should detail the frequency and amount of payments.

» **Occupiers:**
Those questions ask about any current occupiers of the property. The seller needs to list all current occupiers and specify if the arrangements with them are leases or licenses. If the arrangements are leases, then a proper notice will need to be served in order to sell the property with vacant possession.
The sale contract must be signed by the adults occupying the

property to indicate that the property is sold with vacant possession.

» **Services:**

Those questions ask for more details concerning the utilities the property benefits from. The answers should specify if an electrician, whom has been qualified and approved by a relevant professional body, tested the electrical system.

The seller should also specify the type of heating the property uses: gas, electricity, heating oil, etcetera. All installation and maintenance work on the electricity and heating systems must be done according to the Building Regulations. Some of the   questions relate to the presence and maintenance of drainage.

» **Connection to Utilities and Services:**

The seller should state the providers of the different utility services and the location of any meters used to measure the usage of those utilities.

» **Transaction Information:**

Those questions relate to miscellaneous aspects of the transaction: whether the seller is planning on purchasing another property with the proceeds of this sale, whether the proceeds of the sale will be enough to cover the mortgage, whether there are special requirements for the moving day, etcetera.

iii) TA7 & TA9: Leasehold Information Form & Commonhold Information Form

If you are selling the leasehold or the commonhold, you should provide additional information on either the TA7 for leaseholds or the TA9 for commonholds. A sample TA7[15] and TA9[16] form can be found on the website of the Law Society. These forms do not apply to freehold properties.

The form TA7 will require some documentation. The seller

PREPARING TO PURCHASE OR SELL YOUR PROPERTY

of the leasehold needs to provide copies of the lease agreement, of any additional contracts with the management company, of correspondence with the landlord and the management company, of invoices for rent and services charges for the past 3 years, of the building insurance policy and of the constitutional documents of the tenants' management company (if any).

The rest of form TA7 covers general information about any alterations, complains, notices served, maintenance details, etcetera.

The form TA9 asks questions about the Commonhold Association and the seller's interactions with it. The form also covers insurance, complaints, and the rights over the common parts of the property, etcetera.

iv) TA10: Fittings and Contents Form

The TA10[17], along with the TA6[13], will almost always be given to the seller by their legal representative to fill out. A sample TA10[17] form can be found on the website of the Law Society.

The form asks which fittings and fixtures you would like to include with the property.

v) TA13: Completion Information and Undertakings

The form TA13[18] is more technical, although it also includes finalisation details including arrangements to hand over the keys, how and where you will complete, and ensuring that the house is free of all mortgages and liability claims. A sample TA13[18] form can be found on the website of the Law Society.

vi) The Draft Contract

The contract of sale is likely to be based on the Law Society's standard: The Standard Conditions of Sale (fifth edition)[19]. The Law Society is likely to change this edition in the near future.

Your legal representative may use the previously provided

information to amend the standard terms if some terms are inappropriate to the circumstances of your particular transaction.

Your legal representative uses the questionnaire information to draw up a draft contract. This is sent to the buyer for approval.

vii) LPE1

When selling the leasehold or the commonhold, you should provide additional information on the Managing Company and managing agent. The Law Society produced form LPE1 as a standard set of questions in order to facilitate the process of making such inquiries. The form is not compulsory, however it raises the important questions that any standard leasehold transaction would involve. The freehold owners will charge a fee for completing the form. This fee will have to be covered by the seller, who is the leasehold owner.

Of course, this can be a subject of negotiation between the parties and the cost can be passed from the seller to the buyer. This fee can sometimes come as a surprise to the buyer, because he is buying the leasehold interest (i.e. lease of 125-years for £450,000) from the leasehold owner, not from the freehold owner. Thus, paying any fees to the freehold owner is often not an expected expense. The buyer and seller can negotiate who should cover this expense, which currently costs around £400 depending on the managing agent. A sample LPE1[20] form can be found on the website of the Law Society.

viii) Licence to Assign

With a sale of a Leasehold or Commonhold, depending on the provisions of the original lease, the Landlord might need to provide an official Licence to Assign the lease. The requirements for obtaining the Licence to Assign will be described in the lease. The Licence will likely constitute a written approval of the plan to assign the lease to the buyer of the leasehold interest.

6.   THE BUYER'S ROLE

The buyer does not have to complete any of the above forms, although he should be aware and understand what kind of information might be found in them. The legal representative of the buyer needs to examine in details the answers to the forms listed above and report to the buyer in case there are any problems. For example, the seller might indicate in his TA6[13] form that the conservatory that was recently build did not receive planning permission or that there is an on-going dispute with a neighbour about a boundary fence. The buyer needs to decide whether those concerns are serious enough to justify withdrawing from the purchase, or whether the property should be discounted because of an issue.

Another problem might arise if the seller indicates in TA10[17] that he plans on keeping the set of statues that give the garden of your future property the atmosphere you were looking for. In such a case, the buyer should insist on renegotiating with the seller to include those fittings with the sale of the property.

A default in a property may also serve as leverage to renegotiate the asking price. If a house were to have a leaking roof for example, the buyer may be able to ask the seller to lower the selling price of the property to reflect the cost of the repairs the buyer will have to make to the roof.

CHAPTER THREE
Investigation of Title and Pre-Contract Searches

1. THE BUYER: MEETING THE LEGAL REPRESENTATIVE

If you are the buyer, you will normally meet with your legal representative once you have located the property you which to buy, put in an offer and have a mortgage agreement in place. It is possible to do this earlier, however it is more cost effective to do so at this stage. After your legal representative has confirmed your identity, he will ask you for the details of the seller's legal representative.

Once your legal representative knows who they are, your legal representative will write to the seller's legal representative to confirm that they are instructed and request all of the documents we have discussed in Chapter 2. Having received these documents, your legal representative will commence their legal due diligence by first investigating the title to the property.

2. INVESTIGATION OF THE TITLE

As discussed in Chapter 2, the seller's legal representative should have supplied your legal representative with evidence of the seller's title, i.e. an Official copy of register of title, at his or her own expense.

If you are buying the leasehold, then you must receive an official copy of both the leasehold and freehold title. You should also receive a copy of the lease from the seller, as well as documents referred to on the register and any evidence relating to unsettled issues that cannot be clarified by referring to the register. The plans of the property should be included with the official copies.

Your legal representative must then investigate these documents to check that:

a) The seller actually owns the property and is therefore able to sell it; and

b) There are no defects in the title, which would adversely affect your interests or those of your lender.

This is an extremely important part of the conveyancing process because the due diligence provided by your legal representative at this stage should ensure that you know exactly what you are paying for, whether there are hidden expenses attached to the property and, if what comes to light tips the balance, whether you should cut your losses and withdraw from the purchase.

The Official copy of register of title is comprised of 3 parts and a title plan of the land.

The first part is the Property register and it describes the land and estate comprised in the title (i.e. whether it is freehold or leasehold).

The second part is the Proprietorship register and it identifies the owner and specifies the class of the title (e.g. absolute title).

The third part is the Charges register and it lists all of the interests that the property is subject to (e.g. covenants, notices and charges).

a. PROPERTY REGISTER

Firstly, your legal representative will check the Property register to see if the description of the land and its title number corresponds with what is listed in the Draft Contract. The date at the start of the Property register specifies when the title was first registered. There you can also find information about the type of estate you are purchasing: leasehold or freehold. If you are buying the leasehold estate, then there will be short particulars of the lease, including the original parties, the term of the lease and the ground rent. In every Property register you will find a reference to a Title plan, where the extent of the property will be edged in a specific colour (usually red).

Sometimes there might be discrepancies between the actual layout of the property and the Title plan. The legal representatives acting on the transaction very often do not visit the property at all. As a result, it is up to the buyer himself to compare the actual premises with the Title plan upon his visits to the property. If the Title plan is not completely accurate, the buyer should instruct his legal representative to request a revision of the plan.

In the Property register one can also find information about the easements associated with the property. Easements are rights that the property benefits from. Such an easement might be a right of way over a neighbouring property. Not all easements are registered, so your legal representative should contact the seller and enquire about any rights that the property might be enjoying that are not currently listed in the Property register. If there are any such rights, and they have been enjoyed for 40 years without any lawful interruption, then they are deemed absolute. You can continue to enjoy these rights, even though they are not in the Property register.

Finally, in the Property register one can find information whether the property has the benefit of mining rights. Your legal representative should raise inquiries if the property is being sold with the exception of the mining rights. This would indicate that someone else has the right to mine under your property, which can create substantial problems of subsidence. It is advisable to order the appropriate searches (e.g. coal mining search, mining search). Searches are discussed in more detail later in this chapter.

b. PROPRIETORSHIP REGISTER

Secondly, your legal representative will check the Proprietorship Register to see the class of title. There are four classes of title: absolute title, qualified title, possessory title, good leasehold. We will not explore the conditions for the owner to qualify for the specific types of titles, however it is important to note that the different classes give the owner different rights. For example, with an absolute title nobody can challenge your ownership of the property. Furthermore, with that class of title you take the property free of any third-party interests that are not registered in the Charges register (except for some overriding interests which will be discussed below).

It is very important for your legal representative to make enquiries, if there are any problems with the class of title. For example, the owners of qualified and possessory titles can have the land taken away from them, if someone with a better claim to the land challenges their ownership.

Furthermore, the Proprietorship Register will contain any restrictions on the circumstances in which a disposition, (e.g. a sale, mortgage, or gift), can be registered. At this point, an important distinction should be drawn between owning a property as Joint Tenants and as Tenants in Common, which are different types of joint ownership of land.

Joint Tenancy gives each owner an equal right to the whole property. As a result, when one Joint Tenant dies, the property does not pass according to his will or the rules of intestacy, rather it automatically transfers to the other Joint Tenants. On the other hand, if the ownership is as Tenants in Common, the interest of the deceased owner passes according to his will or the rules of intestacy. This has an important implication for who has the legal right to sell the property.

The type of joint ownership will be recorded in the Proprietorship Register of the Official Copy of Register of Title. For example, if the owners of the land hold it as Tenants in Common, as opposed to Joint Tenants, then the following restriction will be seen in the Proprietorship register:

> *"No disposition by a sole proprietor of the registered estate (except a trust corporation) under which capital money arises is to be registered unless authorised by an order of the court."*

As such, the restriction will inform your legal representative as to the procedure that must be followed in order to ensure that your transaction is valid. In the above example, you must get the agreement of all people that hold the interest as Tenants in Common for the transaction to be valid.

The Proprietorship register will also include notices relating to the property. A notice essentially alerts any potential buyers of interests held by third parties in relation to the property. For example, a man or woman, who is separated from their spouse or civil partner without being divorced, may own a property you want to buy. If the spouse or partner's matrimonial home rights[21] have been registered under the charges register, the seller will not be able to sell their property unless written consent is obtained from their partner.

Furthermore, in the Proprietorship register you can sometimes find indemnity covenants. These are binding agreements between two people, which give a certain permanent right to one of them. They are used to pass the obligations of the previous owner to the new owner. For example, person B (the buyer) purchases a residential property and covenants with person A (the seller) not to use it as an office.

However, this covenant is enforceable only against person B, since he was a party to the agreement. If he subsequently sells the property to person C, who converts the property into an office, person A (the original seller) will be able to sue person B (the original buyer) for damages. For that reason, person B would like to include an indemnity covenant in the Proprietorship register, in order to have recourse against person C in the event of a breach of covenant, such as the conversion to an office. This is one example of an indemnity clause:

> *"The Transferee/s hereby covenant/s with the Transferor/s by way of indemnity only to observe and perform the covenants contained or referred to in the registers of title number and to be liable for any future breach or non-observance thereof"*

Such an indemnity clause will make the buyer of the property liable for any future violations of the property restrictions that the previous owners had agreed to. As a result, it is important for your legal representative to take a note of such an indemnity provision.

Finally, for any property that was sold after 12th October 2013, the Proprietorship register should contain information about any chancel repair liability. Such notice determines whether the buyer will be liable to make payments for the repair of the chancel of the local parish.

c. CHARGES REGISTER

Thirdly, your legal representative will check the Charges register to see if there are any covenants, notices and charges. A covenant is a promise to either do or refrain from doing something, (e.g. to maintain a fence or to not build on your land). It is easy to see why you might be concerned about these: imagine you find out that you cannot keep pets or that you have to make regular payments to maintain a fence.

When you are buying the leasehold estate, the holder of the freehold estate might have protected his right to access your property for the purpose of maintaining and renovating neighbouring properties that belong to him. Such a right will be listed in the Charges register. In such a situation, it will be a good idea for your legal representative to make inquiries with the seller about the frequency and nature of such disturbances.

In the Charges register you can also find information about any mortgages that affect the property, or whether it is being used as a security for a loan. It is very important for you to know whether the property is subject to a mortgage or is a security, as that will need to be discharged at the time of completion. Your legal representative will have to raise this issue with the seller and ensure the contract for sale includes provisions stipulating the discharge of the mortgage. The process of completion and mortgage discharge is described in detail in Chapter 7.

3. OVERRIDING INTERESTS

Overriding interests will not be found in the title. For registered land, the general rule is that most interests will be considered binding if they are registered correctly and can be found on the Register of title. Overriding interests are an exception to that rule.

These are interests attached to the land, belonging to other person(s), which will be binding on any subsequent owners, despite the fact that they are not on the register. By 'binding', we mean that the interest must be obeyed in law and is therefore enforceable.

As such, your legal representative may have to investigate beyond the title. If the seller's legal representative obtained details relating to any disadvantageous rights and occupiers' rights if or when they made their own enquiries, they have a duty to disclose such information to you. Failure to disclose such information gives you the right to withdraw from the contract and sue for compensation.

Such an overriding interest can be a short-term lease. Assured Shorthold Tenancies for durations of less than seven years do not have to be registered and will not form a part of the Charges register of the Register of title. However, an Assured Shorthold Tenancy will still be valid once you purchase the property and your new home will not be fully at your disposal. That is why it is very important for your legal representative to make inquiries regarding any Assured Shorthold Tenancy that the property is currently subject to.

Another example of an overriding interest is when you are purchasing a property from a married couple, with the legal title to the property being held by only one of the spouses. If the other spouse had made substantial contributions towards the purchase price of the home, then she would be considered to have a beneficial interest in the property that might be protected by an actual occupation. Such an occupation must be obvious on a reasonably careful inspection of the property. Such factors like paying utility bills, having personal items in the property and visiting it on a daily basis would be sufficient to declare someone to be in actual occupation.

Once again, it is very important for the buyer's legal representative to contact the seller's legal representative and request information about all people with a beneficial interest in the land. Some buyers even visit the property to ascertain whether someone is in actual occupation, such as squatters.

4. ENQUIRIES

Once your legal representative has investigated the Official copy of register of title, they will raise enquiries with the seller's legal representative. The nature of the enquiries will depend on the circumstances of the property (i.e. whether it is freehold or leasehold, whether there are defects in the title, whether the property has undergone any alterations).

Expert's View

Where the buyer is seeking to buy a flat with tenants who remain in occupation, there will be additional enquiries to the standard property enquiries, which will need to be raised with the seller's solicitors. This will include obtaining and reviewing a copy of the current tenancy agreement and raising specific tenancy enquiries to establish the background of the tenant and to ensure that there are no disputes or rent arrears.

The outcome of the title investigation, including the searches and enquiries, will determine whether or not the solicitor is able to provide a clear Report on Title. This is necessary in order to enable the buyer to proceed with the property transaction and onto the next fundamental stage of the conveyancing process: the exchange of contracts.

Philip Li,
Solicitor-Partner

5.   PRE-CONTRACT SEARCHES

After examining the Official copy of register of title, the legal representative of the buyer should order a number of searches to be conducted. It is important to note that the legal representative will rarely be conducting those searches himself. The reason being that the process of ordering searches through local councils will usually be quite complex and time costly. As such legal representative prefer saving both time and money by having specialised professionals conduct these searches. A number of different agencies and organisations can conduct these searches upon receiving instructions from legal representatives. There is a fee for each search requested and the legal representative will pass that cost on to the buyer.

There is a wide range of different searches that can be ordered and it is up to the legal representative to decide which ones are most appropriate.

Expert's View

The most crucial element of buying a property is doing your research. Conducting the right searches is an important step in that direction. The standard bundle we advise people to get is a local search, a drainage search, an environmental search, and a chancel search. Those are the documents, which are standard. There are some other ones such as a coal-mining search, which examines if a property is situated on a coal side. A flood search would indicate the history of flooding in the area. The property doesn't need to be close to a river to be affected. City properties can also be in risk of flooding, depending on the local drainage system. Depending on the location, you might order a HS2 search. The current HS2 scheme has 2 routes and you can get a compulsory purchase order on properties that are on those routes. Generally, you would be quite interested to know if there will be a train passing at 130 miles per hour right next to your property.

Michael Connelly,
Search Agency Director

Next, we will discuss a number of the most common searches and provide important information about each one.

a. LOCAL SEARCH

The local authority search is comprised of three different forms. You can obtain the forms from a law stationary and submit them to the local council however, in the vast majority of cases a specialised company will take care of the procedure.

i) CON29R

This is the main form for establishing whether the property is in breach of regulations. Your legal representative should examine the form carefully to establish if the property has received all planning permissions and building regulations. It is important to collect information about the property in order to know whether there were any alterations or additions that would need such approvals as works are sometimes never declared to the council. The form also informs you if the adjacent roads have been adopted. If a road is adopted, the public authorities maintain it. If it is not adopted – you need to confirm whether you are responsible for its maintenance. The form gives additional information like whether the property is in a conservation area and whether there is any land contamination.

ii) CON29O

This form is optional and would not apply to all property transactions. The form allows you to choose additional questions that the local authority should answer. At the time of writing of this book, each question costs £15, so it is advisable to choose only the ones that you need. The back of the form provides an explanation of the different questions you can ask. You can inquire about any road proposals by private bodies, about restrictions on advertising on the property, about any noise abatement orders the local authority has made and about any common grazing grounds your property might be a part of.

iii) LLC1

This search will reveal any information concerning the property recorded at the Local Land Charges Register. Such information might pertain to anything from a tree preservation order, to money owed to the council.

There is no uniformity among the 353 councils in the UK regarding the cost and processing times of the searches.

Expert's View

Some of the London boroughs take 1 or 2 days to provide the information. We could go to another council and they could take 25-30 working days. When we apply for a regulated search to a council that has adopted the Environment Information Regulation (EIR), they have 20 days to give us the information. Roughly 10% of the councils in the UK, or about 35, work with the EIR. The other councils will respond based on their capabilities. In Birmingham, it takes about 10 working days to get a response. This is most often based on the number of staff and the number of searches they conduct. The price varies as well. For example, council searches in Birmingham are £75, while in Lambeth Council they are about £300.

Michael Connelly,
Search Agency Director

The local authority search might indicate that no building regulation certificates were issued, even though substantial alterations were performed on the property. If the council discovers this omission, it might impose a fine and require additional construction work to be carried out. This is a risk that some homebuyers are not willing to take.

Furthermore, if the buyer requires a mortgage, the lender will require that the appropriate building permits are required. A possible solution is for the parties to take indemnity insurance. It is usually to be negotiated between the seller and the buyer who will pay for the indemnity insurance. The insurance involves making a single payment and the coverage protects the buyer from any cost incurred from actions taken by the council.

Normally, the insurer will require that the alterations were completed at least 12 months before purchasing the insurance. The reason for this requirement is that in most cases the local council has to take actions within 12 months of the completion of the alterations. However, in case the alterations pose a health and safety hazard, the council can take action at any point in time.

Additionally, indemnity insurance can protect a buyer against any violations of Landlord covenants. For example, if you are buying the leasehold estate, the Original lease might have a provision stating that no alteration can be made to the property without the approval of the Landlord. Such alterations can include any building work that will affect the structural integrity of the property. It is possible to purchase insurance coverage that protects the buyer from actions taken by the council, as well as from actions taken by the landlord, in case no such permission was obtained. Insurers that offer indemnity insurance usually offer insurance for indemnity covenants, although it advisable that the buyer raises the issue with the company and get all relevant information.

Indemnity insurances usually stipulate that the policyholder cannot share any information about the alterations with the Local council or the Landlord. The reason for this requirement is that if the Local council finds out about alterations that did not receive Planning permission or Building regulation, and then they might impose a fine or require some remedial work to be completed. Since insurance provider will be liable to cover those expenses, they state that the policyholder cannot inform the relevant bodies about the lack of approval.

b.   ENVIRONMENTAL SEARCH

Those searches use historical records to determine if the property is near contaminated land. Even if there are no clear signs of environmental damage, there might be traces of mercury, lead or arsenic in the ground. Such contamination can pose a serious health hazard to the occupants, so it is very important to conduct an environmental search. Furthermore, if such contamination is discovered after your purchase of the property, you may have to pay for the remediation if the original perpetrator cannot be found. Additionally, the environmental search will give you information about flood risk in the area and about radon contamination. Radon is a radioactive gas that occurs naturally in rocks and soils. It can increase your risk of developing lung cancer, which is another reason to commission an environmental search.

Independent providers who have access to historical records and current sources of contamination conduct the environmental reports.

c.   WATER AND DRAINAGE SEARCH

The form CON29DW gives you a detailed account of the drainage and water facilities servicing the property. It shows you whether the property is connected to a mains water supply. It also shows if the foul water and surface water from the property drain to a public sewer. It also states the providers of those services and the basis for charges. This report also contains more useful information, such as the risk of low water pressure and of internal flooding.

d.   CHANCEL SEARCH

If your property is in a church parish, you might be liable to pay for certain repairs that might be needed to the church. A Chancel search will indicate if your intended property is within such a parish. It is very difficult to predict if such a repair expense will arise in the future, so it may be advisable to buy chancel insurance that will cover the cost of any repair liability up to a certain amount.

It should also be noted that for any property that was sold after 12th October 2013, any chancel repair liability should be registered as a notice in the Proprietorship register of the register of title. Thus, a buyer should be able to find out whether he is liable to pay for chancel repair from examining the title document of the property.

e.   COAL MINING SEARCH

A coal-mining search is advisable if you know that the property is situated in a coal region. The report will give you information about any mine entries within 20 metres of the property and any subsidence hazards. It will also show information about any coal-related gas emissions and water contamination. The source of that information is the Coal Authority[22], which has detailed accounts on any mining legacy issues. The authority will also have information about any future mining plans in the region.

Expert's View

Usually, the solicitor of the buyer will approach us with questions about a specific property. Once we have the location, we will check our interactive risk map to determine if it is in a mining risk zone. If it is, we will proceed with a search of numerous historical records to assess the risk of all nearby mining. We will present a 3-4-page report to the solicitor identifying different risks. If there is a substantial risk – for example, there is a tin mine shaft within the property and no clear records that the shaft was sealed or secured – we will recommend a site investigation. If the owner of the property agrees, we will visit the site and perform a drilling survey. If the results of the survey identify mine workings, we will advise on the type of remedial activity that needs to be undertaken – often this involves employing the services of structural engineers to secure the mine workings.

Paul Raglan,
Mining Search Agency Director

f.   MINING SEARCHES

Coal mining is not the only relevant risk factor, when it comes to mining operations. Prospective buyers need to be aware of several different mining risks associated with other types of mines.

Expert's View

Until relatively recently, mining search risks were sometimes overlooked. The effects of this can be disastrous – only recently a chalk mine was found under a school causing the site to be evacuated. That is why it is important to examine the full spectrum of mining risks – metal, limestone, chalk, coal, etc. In the worst cases – mine workings have caused buildings to collapse. Often, there is substantial physical damage done to the property as a result of subsidence – a corner of the house simply collapses in to the ground. Myself and other members of my team have over 25 years of experience in identifying mining-related problems. Once we identify a risk remedial costs can be considered.

Paul Raglan,
Mining Search Agency Director

g.   HS2 SEARCH

The High Speed 2 project is a high-speed railway that links London with Leeds and Manchester, through Birmingham. Work on the project is scheduled to begin in mid-2017 and the final stages should be completed by 2033. While there currently are plans for the precise routes, they have not been finalised yet. Thus, it is advisable to check if the proposed routes will affect the property you are buying, by going to the government HS2 web-page[23].

6.   SEARCH RESULTS

It is very important for the legal representative of the buyer to examine in detail the results of the different reports. If any substantial issues arise from the reports, the legal representative should take the appropriate actions.

The possible courses of action differ based on the information received. For example, difficulties arising from a missing building regulation certificate can be overcome by purchasing insurance. On the other hand, there is little the buyer can do about mercury poisoning in the soil under a house. Possible remediation activities might be prohibitively expensive. The presence of an active mine in the vicinity of the property is another problem that will be difficult to resolve. In such scenarios, the legal representative should discuss the problems with the buyer. At this point, the buyer should conduct a cost-benefit analysis to determine if he should continue with the purchase of the property.

7.   SEARCH AGENCIES

There is an overwhelming amount of information that needs to be considered in the process of conducting property searches. Search agencies can facilitate this process greatly and ensure that you conduct the right searches and at affordable prices.

Search agencies are best suited for identifying the various searches that are necessary to the property at hand. Through their records, they will be able to tell if the property is situated in a mining region or that nearby properties have had problems with mercury contamination for example.

These records are created through the conduct of numerous searches, which enables them to create databases of key points that need to be included in each search. Furthermore, they are sometimes integrated with other agencies to landmark vital information. When a property is specified through a search agent, a number of search recommendations would appear. Those are specifically tailored to the property, based on information from related property searches and key guidelines provided by agencies. As a result, search agencies can give valuable information about the most appropriate searches that should be conducted for a specific property.

The process of ordering searching from a number of different councils and agencies can be time-consuming. Ordering the full bundle from a few different providers can also be very costly. Councils have their own specific ways of reporting information in response to searches. If a legal representative is ordering a search from a council that he has never worked with before, he might be exposed to a new format of reporting. Search agencies have standardised formats of reporting, which means that reports from any council will be presented to the legal representative in the same format. For those reasons, legal representatives are increasingly turning to search agencies for their search needs.

Expert's View

It is still commonplace for solicitors to go directly to the Local Authority, the Drainage and Water Company, the Environmental Agency, or the Coal Company. However, we give them a very simple

*platform to do all that. If a solicitor was to draw up
those documents separately, it would probably take
them about 15 – 20 minutes to place a search bundle.
If they go on-line and use our services – it will take
them 1 minute.*

*Due to the volume of searches we do, we get
massive discounts that are not offered to the solicitor
that is doing 30 – 40 bundles a month. Generally, we
offer the same products at cheaper prices and we get
a quicker turnaround time. Finally, we can back-up
all the information for up to 7 years. So, if their
system is down or their data is corrupted, then they
can request the data from us.*

Michael Connelly,
Search Agency Director

Furthermore, some search agencies have different insurances to
cover omissions. Search agencies need to have professional
indemnity insurance that covers any mistakes that they might
make in the process of collecting the search information. Some
agencies have an additional insurance to cover mistakes that the
council might make in the process of conducting the searches.
Such insurance can save you both time and money, because
without it you will have to litigate against the council in order to
hold them responsible for the mistake.

Expert's View

*We have 2 insurances in place. As per compliance
regulations, we have a £2 million professional
indemnity insurance to cover for errors or omissions
that may be made by us. In addition to that, for any
of the regulated products that we supply, we have a
£2 million specialist search insurance that will cover*

for errors or omissions made by the council. For example, if they are holding a planning entry against the incorrect property or they have missed a planning entry from a property. A solicitor can approach us within 6 months of the transaction and state the problem – for example a building regulation was never issued, contrary to what the council stated. At this stage, we will check with the council whether the information they provided was indeed incorrect. If it was, then the insurance will cover the related cost of our client. If the client had gone directly to the council for a council search, then their only option would be to sue the council directly.

Michael Connelly,

Search Agency Director

Whilst your legal representative would traditionally be the one to order the searches, is not the only party that can request the services of a search agent, such as iCompile Searches. Now a day, an individual who is looking to buy a property can also approach the search agencies. This may save time, as your legal representative will usually order those searches only after you have engaged him and have paid him.

It can also be beneficial to know about any serious problems with the property before you have engaged the services of a legal representative. In that way, you can start looking for another property without having paid any legal fees. However, one must bear in mind that the searches will need to have been recent in order to be used by the legal representative. If you have ordered a search on the property several months before the start of the conveyancing process, your legal representative may be required to reorder these searches to ensure that they are still accurate.

8.   SURVEYS

A building survey is the most detailed house survey that can be ordered and focuses on the condition of the property. Ordering such a survey is recommended for certain types of properties. If you are buying an older house or one that has been altered significantly, it is advisable to conduct a building survey that will confirm the condition of the home. Such a survey will list the visible defects and the hidden flaws with references to specific repair options. The survey can be tailored to examine specific areas of concern, based on the requirements of the buyer. Such a survey is appropriate when you are considering making changes to the layout of the property.

It is important to instruct the right surveyor for the survey of the property. Many factors can be taken into consideration, like credentials, experience and costs.

Expert's View

When a survey or a valuation is required – it should be done properly and with appropriate detail regardless of whether the final fee is £2,000 or £5,000. A detailed survey or valuation should always be carried out professionally, slowly and efficiently. In particular and when possible communication between client and surveyor should be made before the inspection to discuss and ascertain precisely what is expected and required. It is not a matter of doing things cheaply and as quickly as possible. Quoting a fixed price for performing a building survey can be difficult, because it depends on many variables relating to the size, use, value, situation, age, accessibility, locality and condition of the property.

On valuations, if a valuation is done for

obtaining a mortgage, (for secured lending purposes) the fee may be much higher than if it was done for trust, pension, company or any other non-secured lending purposes depending on liabilities involved. Speed may or may not be something to consider. Generally, clients may wish to have the survey and valuation done as soon as possible, but may have to consider both the time schedule of the surveyor and the legal aspect of the transaction. Sometimes surveyors may postpone the survey or valuation until the solicitors have finalised the sale agreement.

Malcolm Marsdin,
Chartered Surveyor and RICS Registered Valuer

While the price should not be the decisive factor when ordering a survey, the qualifications of the surveyor should be. It is advisable to use the services of a Chartered Surveyor, who will be a member of the Royal Institute of Chartered Surveyors[7]. This designation is a sign for both the expertise and experience a surveyor has. To become a Chartered Surveyor, a person needs four years of university education and between two and three years of structured training with a registered surveyor. Thus, the designation is an indication that a person is qualified, experienced and trustworthy enough to be a surveyor.

It is important to note that if a surveyor conducts a building survey, they can be held liable for any omissions that would have been apparent on a reasonable inspection - for example, missing a large crack on an outside retaining wall. RICS[7] requires surveyors to have professional liability insurance, which will cover instances of professional negligence. You are advised to consult with your legal representative if you think the survey was not of a satisfactory quality.

CHAPTER FOUR
Before Exchange

Once the buyer's legal representative has investigated the title and has received the results of all the necessary searches, he will then proceed to raising enquiries and additional enquiries with the seller's legal representative. Once it has been compiled, this information will form part of the Report on Title that the legal representative of the buyer will send to his client. After that report is presented to the buyer, the parties will continue with the exchange of contracts, at which point the contract between the seller and buyer becomes binding.

In short, the point of exchange equates to a point of no return. If one party attempts to withdraw from the transaction after exchange, this will amount to a breach of contract. The other party will be able to rely on that breach to sue for compensation. Because of the binding nature of the exchange, the legal representative of the buyer must raise all relevant questions before the exchange of contracts.

Expert's View
Once they have received the results of all the property searches, as well as full replies to our pre-contract and additional enquiries, your solicitor will

review the information and will highlight any matters or issues of concern which are likely to impact upon your decision to proceed with the purchase.

If any issues or problems are identified, your solicitor will endeavour to find a solution or to carry out such further investigative work as is necessary in order to determine whether the problem is one, which can be remedied, allowing the buyer to proceed, or whether the problem is such that there is no acceptable solution available. In such instances, the buyer will be advised not to proceed.

At this stage, the buyer will have an opportunity to discuss the results of the legal due diligence with the solicitor, to enable them to clarify any aspects of the title investigation which the buyer may not fully understand.

Philip Li,
Solicitor-Partner

1.   THE SELLER: PRE-EXCHANGE

There are a number of matters that the seller's legal representative should review before proceeding to exchange. If the transaction is not proceeding according to expectation, you should ask your legal representative what is causing the delay. Once you know the cause, you might be able to start pressing the relevant party to take action in respect of the issue or simply ask your legal representative if there are anything you could do to help.

Prior to exchange, your legal representative may be dealing with the following:

»   Enquiries and Additional Enquiries
»   The Draft Contract

»   Mortgage Arrangements
»   The Deposit & Insurance
»   Synchronisation

a. ENQUIRIES AND ADDITIONAL ENQUIRIES

It is of extreme importance that the seller adequately responds to the buyer's enquiries and discloses to the buyer latent defects. By 'latent', it is meant that the defect is not apparent on a reasonable inspection of the land. By 'defect', we are referring to some flaw in the property. However, it is unclear as to what criteria are used to determine whether a defect is latent or patent.

In Yandle & Sons v Sutton, the existence of a public footpath across the land being bought was deemed to be a latent defect in the title, i.e. the right of way or 'easement' meant that the owner of the land was obliged to let people use his land for a specific purpose: in this instance, to cross from one side to the other.

This easement was arguably obvious to an individual inspecting the land, however it was nonetheless deemed to be a latent defect. Thus, it was found that the buyer was entitled to 'rescind' the contract, i.e. withdraw from and undo the contract, because the seller had not disclosed the latent defect. As such, a prudent seller should seek to disclose all defects: both unprompted and in response to the buyer's enquiries.

If a defect in title is found which cannot be resolved, your legal representative may recommend that you acquire defective title insurance to cover any liability stemming from the defect. For example, the previous leasehold owners removed a wall in the apartment. However, the property's title may include a covenant that prohibits making any structural changes to the property, without the consent of the Landlord. The appropriate indemnity insurance can protect you against any claims by the Landlord.

For guidance regarding this particular issue, you should seek out the professional advice of your legal representative.

b. THE DRAFT CONTRACT

As already mentioned, the seller's legal representative would have sent a draft contract to the buyer's legal representative at the beginning of the conveyancing process. Depending on the results of the searches and enquiries they made, the buyer's legal representative may then write to the seller's legal representative to discuss amendments to the Draft Contract.

For instance, they may wish to discuss the items on the list of fixtures and fittings: the seller's legal representative may argue that a certain item is a fixture and therefore part of the sale. The two parties should negotiate over what furniture and appliances will pass to the buyer and the final agreement should be included in the contract. Following the inclusion of all the agreed amendments, both legal representatives will check to see that their respective copies are identical.

The seller's legal representatives will send the Official Copy of the Register of Title with the contract pack to the buyer's legal representatives. The contract will refer specifically to that Official Copy, by referencing its number and the date on which it was obtained. The Official Copy of the Title plan that outlines the boundaries of the property will usually be attached as well.

As the parties negotiate, certain changes will be made to the Draft contract. Sometimes, for convenience, the parties will include changes to the contract as a separate "Rider" clause in the end of the contract. Including another clause in the existing contract might create formatting difficulties, especially if the contract is long and contains numerous references. As a result, any additions added later in the contract can simply be appended as a Rider clause. An example of this may be a clause including the sale of certain pieces of furniture along with the property.

Another common rider in sales of Leaseholds is the addition

of a retention clause. The buyer's legal representatives would ask that a reasonable amount of funds from the monies to be transferred on completion be put aside by the seller's legal representatives in case of any outstanding charges (such as service charge or ground rent) that the seller was responsible for paying. This amount is typically between £500 and £1000. After an agreed period of time (usually 6-12 months), if no charge has come up, the seller's legal representatives would transfer the retained amount to the seller.

Once both parties have agreed to the contract's terms, the buyer's legal representative will then return the approved draft contract to the seller's legal representative, who will explain the terms to his client.

The draft contract can include hand-written amendments, as long as the parties agree over those amendments. Usually the date of the contract will be written by hand at the time of signing. However, it is not unusual for other provisions to be included by hand – for example the parties might decide to include the final price at the time of signing, at which point the price will be hand manuscript.

Last minute amendments, such as a rider, can always be added after the contract has been signed (but before exchange) as long as you have instructed your legal representative to do so and the changes have been agreed to by both parties.

c. MORTGAGE ARRANGEMENTS

The buyer's legal representative should notify the seller's legal representative whether the buyer would be relying on a mortgage. This information should be communicated from the very beginning of the transaction, because the legal representative of the lender will be making inquiries from the seller throughout the transaction.

If the buyer is relying on a mortgage, the seller's legal

representative may check the validity of the buyer's mortgage offer as such offers will invariably have an expiry date. This is particularly important if the property being sold is a new build property as they will invariably be in the course of construction.

It is difficult to accurately predict when a new build property will be finished due to a few possible reasons (e.g. adverse weather conditions, delays in materials being delivered, planning issues). If the mortgage offer expires before completion, the buyer might be forced to reapply for an alternative mortgage offer.

More commonly, the property you wish to sell may have an existing mortgage attached to it. In such instances, the seller's legal representative would need to take steps towards the discharge of the mortgage, such as requesting a quote for the exact amount that must be redeemed on the mortgage from the bank/building society, also known as a redemption statement.

d. THE DEPOSIT & INSURANCE

Your legal representative may double-check to see how much the buyer will need to provide towards the deposit upon exchange and to whom. As already discussed in Chapter 1, the amount of the deposit may vary greatly, however it is usually 10%. If the buyer has requested that you accept a reduced deposit, your legal representative must explain to you the potential consequences of taking such a deposit and have your written consent before agreeing to take such a deposit.

Assuming that you have an insurance policy over the property you wish to sell, it may also be necessary to contact the providers of your insurance policy if the buyer wishes to rely on the same policy. This is in order for their interest to be noted on that policy.

e. SYNCHRONISATION

Synchronisation is the process of simultaneous exchange and

completion on two related sales of property. If you are financing the purchase of your property with the proceeds of the sale of your current home, then it is important to have the two transactions executed simultaneously.

If you manage to sell your property before finalising the related purchase, you are risking having to find a temporary residence. On the other hand, if the sale of your current property is being delayed, then you are risking losing the new property you have chosen.

Expert's View

It is very common for buyers who are not first-time buyers to have to rely upon the sale of an existing property in order to fund the purchase of their new property. This is called a related sale. Insofar as the conveyancing process is concerned, there is no difference in the way the legal due diligence needs to be carried out in relation to both the purchase and sale transaction.

The key to ensuring that there is both a satisfactory, simultaneous exchange and completion depends on the solicitor acting for the buyer or seller: whether they can manage the expectations of all the parties in the chain transaction, as well as to manage the files in such a way that the legal due diligence is carried out and concluded at the same time so as to allow a simultaneous exchange and a simultaneous completion on the agreed date.

Philip Li,
Solicitor-Partner

Your legal representative will then need to ensure that the timing of your two property transactions is synchronised before going forward with the exchange of contracts. However, this may be more complex and take more time depending on how many related sales are involved, i.e. how long the property chain is.

2. THE BUYER: PRE-EXCHANGE

The responsibility of raising requisitions lies with the buyer. The buyer's legal representative will not only have to review the issues discussed by the seller's legal representative, he will also have a number of additional issues to raise:

» Enquiries
» Requisitions on Title
» The Contract
» Mortgage Arrangements
» The Deposit & Insurance
» Synchronisation
» Completion Arrangements
» Method of Exchange
» Occupiers

We will describe some of these elements in the subsequent chapters.

a. ENQUIRIES

While the seller has a duty to disclose all latent defects, this duty does not extend to any physical or patent defects in the property. This relates to the principle of caveat emptor, which we discussed in Chapter 2. It states that the responsibility for discovering any physical or patent defects in the property lies with the buyer.

It is for this reason that the buyer should, as a general rule, always inspect the property before buying. Undoubtedly, you would have already done this in your own capacity, however it is a good idea to do so again once you have met with your legal representative as they may have made you aware of any legal issues relating to the property.

In Chapter 2 we described a number of different forms that the seller will have to provide to the buyer (i.e. TA6[13], TA10[17], LPE1[20]). At this stage, the buyer's legal representative should have received the completed forms. Additionally, in Chapter 3 we discussed several different searches and surveys that the buyer's legal representative should commission. At this stage, the buyer's legal representative should collect and examine all the information obtained in through questionnaires and searches. This information should enable him to form an accurate understanding of any problem areas that need to be discussed with the seller.

Having the above information will enable the buyer's legal representative to raise enquiries with the seller's legal representative. There are a vast number of questions that can be raised here. We have grouped some important questions below, based on types of property your legal representatives will ask for:

Leases:
» The Memorandum and Articles of Association of the Tenants Association;
» The person/company to contact to obtain a new share certificate;
» The original share certificate to be provided on completion together with a stock transfer form;
» The Managing Company's leasehold information pack;
» The service costs payable to any Managing Company over the past 3 years;

Commonhold:
» The Memorandum and Articles of Association of the Commonhold Association;
» The person/company to contact to obtain a new share certificate;
» The original share certificate to be provided on completion together with a stock transfer form;

General:

» The full details of any charges over the property;

» Any changes of the lenders holding charges over the property;

» Details of the insurance, whose responsibility it is, and proofs of existing coverage;

» The Gas Safety Record;

» Copies of Planning permissions, Building regulation approvals, and Completion certificates;

» An Energy Performance Certificate;

» Confirmation the seller's identify was verified;

Properties with Tenants:

» The information about current leases of the property: term, rate, and conditions;

» A Tenancy agreement, Tenancy Deposit Scheme, and Draft Rent authority letter;

» Confirmation that there have been no disputes with the Tenants or difficulties in collecting rent;

» An undertaking to assign the deposit account to the buyer;

» Confirmation of whether there is an agency involved in the tenancy;

» Confirmation of who owns the furniture: Landlord or Tenant.

This list is by no means exhaustive, although it raises some of the standard requisitions that need to be answered in order to protect the interest of the buyer.

Expert's View

One important requisition is concerning extensions and alterations. We often ask our client at the time when we carry out our due diligence whether they have inspected the property and if so whether they can identify any alterations or additions that have been carried out to the property. For example, loft conversions and side extensions. We ask such question to establish whether or not these works require building regulation consent and/or planning permission.

Another example is service charges. When you are acquiring an apartment in a block, one of the key questions we ask the managing agent is whether there are there any works planned which are likely to increase the Service charge liability?

When you put an offer on a property, the service charges may be advertised as "£2,000 per annum" for example, however, this is usually an estimate only. This does not specify whether the management company or the freeholder are planning any substantial works which is likely to increase the service charges for the period of the works as soon as you move in. Examples of major works include replacing the roof, repainting the exterior of the block or essential repairs to the structure of the property. Hence, we always recommend a survey is organised to identify any disrepair in the building which may require works.

Philip Li,
Solicitor-Partner

There are many other questions that can be raised following the examination of the search results. Those searches were discussed in detail in Chapter 3 and some of the possible questions were raised there. Here is a list of some additional questions that your legal representatives will ask for (bear in mind this list it not exhaustive):

Local Authority Search:

» Whether any additions, alterations or major renovations have been conducted, besides the ones listed by the Local Authority;

» Copies of all Competent Persons' Certificates applicable to the property;

» Copies of the FENSA certificates for windows and doors;

Environmental:

» Knowledge of any activities involving hazardous substances in the area;

» Details on the quality of air and water in the area;

» Details on any flooding in the area after heavy rainfalls;

Water and Drainage:

» Knowledge of any disruptions in the water and drainage services;

» Knowledge of any recent renovations of the public sewers;

» Knowledge of any problems with the water pressure;

It is important to note that if the buyer is financing the purchase with a mortgage, the bank or building society providing the mortgage will make numerous requisitions about the property. As a result, the buyer will have to raise certain questions, for his own protection, and for receiving mortgage approval.

The legal representatives of the lender will be focusing mainly on problems that relate to the legal title of the property and to any third-party interests over the property (e.g. other lenders, tenants, other owners). It is important to keep in mind that the buyer's interests do not coincide completely with the lender's interests. As a result, while the buyer must raise the questions required by the lender, he must also raise other important questions that relate to his interest in the property.

The requirements of the lender are discussed in more detail in the section on Mortgage arrangements on the next page.

b. REQUISITIONS ON TITLE

The official copy of register of title was discussed in detail in Chapter 3. The Property, Proprietorship and Charges registers can point your legal representative to raise numerous questions relating to the property.

Property Register:

»   Are there any previous leases that can be identified?

»   What are the natures of the easements (covered in Chapter 3) that benefit the property?

»   Are there any easements that are not included in the register?

Proprietorship Register:

»   Are there any problems with the class of title?

»   Who are all the Tenants in Common?

»   Are there any third-party interests as indicated by a notice?

»   Who are the beneficiaries of any indemnity covenants?

Charges Register:

»   Have outstanding charges been redeemed?

»   What is the cost and frequency of any maintenance obligations?

»   What is the nature of any third-party rights over the property?

Those are all important questions that might need to be raised, based on the information found in the register of title.

c. THE CONTRACT

The details relating to the work required by the buyer's legal representative, in respect of the contract, do not differ from those relating to the work of the seller's legal representative, as discussed above. Generally, the two parties need to come to an agreement about the provisions of the contract.

While the price is probably already agreed upon, the parties should negotiate over additional expenses, furniture and appliances, insurance coverage, and exact time and date of completion. The buyer should bear in mind when the mortgage financing will be released and completing before that date will likely be impossible. The precise timing of completion can also be a relevant negotiation point. The default time in the Standard Conditions of Sale (Fifth edition)[19] is 2PM, however this can be changed if the buyer does not think the payment can be sent before that time.

Once the two parties have agreed on the aspects of the contract, both legal representatives will make sure each side has the latest copy and that all the relevant information is correct.

d.   MORTGAGE ARRANGEMENTS

Before your legal representative can advise you to exchange contracts, they must ensure that you have a mortgage offer in place and, where necessary, that you have accepted it. As already discussed, mortgage offers do expire, so it is important to be mindful of the deadline for completing the transaction.

If you have yet to accept your mortgage offer, your legal representative will advise you about the conditions attached to the offer, the terms of the mortgage and your ability to comply with those terms.

Even if you have formally accepted your mortgage offer, a lender may be entitled to withdraw their offer if a condition of theirs is not complied with. This can apply even after contracts have been exchanged.

Given this fact, your legal representative will determine whether you can comply with the attached conditions and will advise you accordingly. Common conditions include a requirement not to let the property without first obtaining the lender's consent, however there may also be special conditions relating to your particular mortgage. For instance, your mortgage may have a condition that a stated sum is retained from the mortgage advance until repairs have been carried out, or a condition requiring the borrower to acquire a new endowment policy as security for the mortgage.

Should your legal representative deem the condition(s) attached to be less than completely satisfactory, they may attempt to negotiate those conditions with the lender. However, if you have opted to instruct a legal representative from your lender's panel, then your legal representative cannot negotiate on your behalf as this would amount to a conflict of interests.

If you have accepted the mortgage offer, your legal representative should ensure that arrangements are in place to comply with any conditions attached. Lenders will require a list of documents to be supplied to them before exchange takes place. The buyer's legal representative would have obtained most of those documents already: i.e. the searches described in Chapter 3, the questionnaires and the Official copy of the Title Register described in Chapter 2.

The following is a list of documents a lender might require before contracts are exchanged. The list is not exhaustive, however it covers the usual requirements that lenders have:

» Copy of the certified proofs of identification and residence of the borrower;
» Copy of the approved sale contract;
» Official Copies of the Register and Title Plan (not more than 6 months old);
» Copies of the replies to the Property Information Form and Leasehold Information Form;
» Copy of the Local Authority Search;
» Copies of all indemnity policies;
» Copies of all Planning Permissions and Building Regulation Approvals;
» Copy of the settled Transfer Deed;
» Energy Performance Certificate;

If the property being purchased is leasehold, then there might be some additional requirements by the lender:

» Official Copy of the Lease
» Deeds of Variation to the original lease;
» Memorandum and Articles of Association of any management company;
» Last 3 years' service charge accounts;
» Landlord and/or Management Company's leasehold information pack.

Once again, the buyer would have obtained most of these documents and raised some of these questions in the process of conducting the due diligence on the property. The fact that lenders also require that information only serves to prove how important the requisitions listed above are.

While the buyer already has a mortgage offer, those documents need to be supplied to the lender in order for the funds to be advanced. Those Pre-exchange requirements are not the only conditions the lender will have – usually lenders have a separate set of documents required for the Pre-completion and the Post-completion stage. Those will be discussed in the subsequent chapters that describe the processes of Pre- and Post-completion.

e.   THE DEPOSIT & INSURANCE

Your legal representative will check that your proposed financial arrangements are in order.

Where the transaction is part of a chain of transactions, it is not uncommon for sellers further up the chain to accept a deposit of less than 10% on the basis that the full purchase price will be available on completion because the sale proceeds and mortgage funding only become available at that date. It is also possible for the parties to agree that on exchange the deposits arc to be held to order pending completion. This means each legal representative in the chain holds their client's deposit in their client account, strictly to the order of the seller's legal representative, and transfers the full purchase price on completion.

If you engage in a related sale which is not synchronized, you may have to pay a deposit for the new property before the proceeds of the sale of your old property are available. As a result, you might need a bridging loan to cover that gap.

The lender of a bridging loan will often require an undertaking, which is a promise to do or refrain from doing something, from the buyer's legal representative. With regards to a bridging loan, the buyer's legal representative would undertake to repay the loan, usually from the proceeds of the sale.

f.   SYNCHRONISATION

As explained above, the issue of synchronisation affects both buyers and sellers. You should consider some factors before engaging in a related transaction.

Expert's View
Some words of advice:

1.   Try not to put an offer on a property that has a long chain - it is one of a number of properties which need to be purchased and sold simultaneously by numerous buyers and sellers. The longer the chain the more likely there will be delays and the risk of the chain collapsing;

2.   Do your research on the Buyers and Sellers in the chain to find out whether there are any factors, which may impact upon their own ability to proceed (e.g. do they need a mortgage offer, are they relying on funds from a third party, the reasons why they are buying and selling);

3.   Ensure that your funding is in place at the outset so that you have the ability to complete the purchase of the property. You do not want any delays on your purchase transaction affecting your sale.

4. Avoid buying new build Property (where you have to sell your existing property in order to buy a replacement home) unless the property is structurally complete and the Developer can agree a fixed completion date. It is always difficult to agree a fixed completion date when the development is still under construction and this may deter a buyer of the property you are selling.

5. Ensure you have a contingency in place in case you are not able to exchange and complete simultaneously due to reasons outside your control, for example, another party in the chain is unable to complete for whatever reason. You should ensure that you have somewhere to stay on a temporary basis and the removals company can store your belongings and effects until such time as you are ready to complete.

Philip Li,
Solicitor-Partner

3. THE REPORT ON TITLE

We have detailed numerous stages at which the legal representative of the buyer is collecting information about the property. After receiving and examining the information from the Title documents, the searches, the surveys, the mortgage documents (if applicable), the questionnaires and the additional requisitions, the buyer's legal representative will list all the relevant details in a report to his client.

If the legal representative is certain that the proposed financial arrangements are in order for the purchase of the property, they will proceed to prepare and present to the buyer a report on the proposed purchase, commonly referred to as the 'Report on Title'. The report will also include information on the different expenses incurred in the process of collecting the information and on the expected future expenses: e.g. cost of searches, cost of surveys, cost of future SDLT payment, cost of future Land Registry application.

Expert's View

The Report on Title is submitted to the buyer before contracts are exchanged and thus before the Buyer is legally committed to the purchase. It is usual for the Report to be submitted to the buyer as soon as the legal due diligence has been fully carried out.

Its purpose is to provide an overview of the due diligence process and to report any issues to the buyer upon which they would need to make a decision. The buyer would then proceed based on the Report and their decision.

Usually, the Report on Title is submitted to the buyer together with the purchase contract for signature. At that point, the solicitor would then require the buyer to pay a 10% deposit, which would be required before contracts are exchanged.

A typical Report on Title will contain the following:

» *Details of the Property (including a full postal address, a plan and whether it is freehold or leasehold);*

» *Details of any matters benefitting or burdening the Property;*

» *Purchase Price and a summary of the contract terms;*

» *Terms of any proposed mortgage (including any conditions attached to the mortgage offer);*
» *Results of the property searches;*
» *A summary of the important replies to pre-contract enquiries;*
» *Details of any planning permissions and building regulation consents the Property has the Benefit of;*
» *A reminder to put into place building insurance (where applicable); and*
» *A summary of the principal terms of the lease (where the property is a leasehold property).*

Philip Li,
Solicitor-Partner

CHAPTER FIVE
The Exchange of Contracts

1. BEFORE EXCHANGE

The buyer's legal representative should confirm that his client has reviewed and approved the Report on Title that was sent after the completion of the searches and requisitions. The draft contract is enclosed with the Report on Title and the buyer should examine all the documents in detail. If the buyer is satisfied with the conditions of the draft contract and the description of the property in the Report on Title, he will instruct his legal representative to proceed with the exchange of contracts.

An important step at this point is for the buyer's legal representative to receive the deposit from his client, as the deposit will be payable on the date of exchange of contracts. Legal representatives will not be able to pay for the deposit out of their own funds. Once the deposit has been transferred to the client account of the firm representing the buyer, they can proceed with the exchange.

If the buyer is involved in a chain of property transactions that are not synchronised and has not yet completed the sale of his property, it is at this stage that a bridging loan could be considered if needed. These loans were already mentioned in Chapter 4. The main purpose they serve is to allow the buyer to pay the deposit, even though he has not yet received the proceeds from selling his own home. Once the buyer sells his old property, he will have to use the proceeds to redeem the bridging loan. Of course, the balance left of the proceeds will be used towards the purchase of the new property. It is important to note that these loans are often offered with higher interest than normal mortgages. As such you may wish to strongly consider all of your options before using a bridging loan.

Naturally, the seller's legal representative should also have sent the draft contract to their client by this stage. If the seller has approved the draft contract and instructed their legal representatives, they can proceed with the exchange.

Each of the legal representatives should have the contract, signed by his client, ready for exchange. If both representatives have the signed contracts in their possession, they can exchange at the earliest possible convenience and avoid any last-minute delays because of a lack of client signature.

2. WHY EXCHANGE?

For exchange to take place, two identical contracts are prepared: one requiring the seller's signature and the other requiring the buyer's signature or the signatures of their respective legal representatives. Additionally, the deposit will need to be transferred to the legal firm representing the seller by either check, bank transfer, or by being "held to order" (this term will be explained later on in this chapter).

It is important to be certain of the terms of the contract in order to prevent any misunderstanding between the parties. Additionally, the contract can be used later on to settle a point of dispute between the parties, so it is crucial for the provisions to be clear. The contract comes into force at the time of exchange, which is agreed between the parties.

Exchange is particularly important when there is a

significant gap between the date of completion and exchange as it provides security for both the seller and the buyer. Once the contracts have been exchanged, and the deposit transferred the contract becomes a binding contract.

After this point the buyer will have to forfeit his deposit if he wishes to pull out of the purchase and both parties will be able to serve a notice to complete onto the other party if the completion date is pushed back. It is important to note that past this stage, if the seller were to drop out of the sale, they would be responsible for the costs incurred by the buyer with regards to the sale and may even be liable for securing the buyers temporary accommodation should he need some.

Both parties can chose to sign the same contract. However, because it is simpler and faster for each party to sign their respective contracts, it is usual to have two separate contracts each with one signature.

Where contracts are exchanged, it is crucial that the two documents contain the same clauses and the same date of completion. The contract will not be binding should the contracts contain different provisions, even if exchange has occurred.

Whether you are buying or selling, your legal representative will likely carry out the exchange on your behalf. They must do so with your express authority. Once express authority is obtained, it has been held that your legal representative has the capacity to affect the exchange using what they think will be the most suitable method.

3. SIGNATURE

Before exchange can take place, the contracts must be signed. It is always advisable for a person to sign their own contract, as they are the contracting party. However, if the circumstances require it, the buyer/seller can authorise their legal representative's firm to sign the contract in their name. Such a step should be taken with caution, as it gives the legal representative the power to sign a contract with the other party in the transaction. A buyer or seller can give such an authority in writing to their legal representative.

The authorisation will be limited in scope to that specific property transaction – it will not give the legal representatives the power to sign other contracts on behalf of their client. Furthermore, the person that granted it can revoke the authorisation.

Some legal representatives are not willing to be authorised to sign contracts and insist on having the client sign the contract himself. This is taken as precautions against potential identify fraud.

It is important to note that non-owning occupiers should also sign the contract. Overriding interests were discussed in the previous chapters of this book, with one such interest relating to people in actual occupation. In order to buy the property free of the interests of people in actual occupation, the buyer should ensure that all people that are in actual occupation sign the contract. For example, if a house is legally owned by the husband, with the wife having also made financial contributions towards the property and is currently living in the property, her signature will be required for selling the house.

4. METHODS OF EXCHANGE

There are several methods of exchanging contracts in residential property transactions. While the legal representatives are the parties responsible for the exchange, it is useful for buyers and sellers to be aware of the procedure to anticipate possible difficulties and provide all necessary information.

There are 4 widely recognized methods of exchanging contracts:

» exchange in person;
» exchange by post;

»   exchange by telephone; and

»   exchange by fax/e-mail.

Furthermore, The Law Society[24] has developed three methods for exchanging contracts over the telephone.

In residential property transactions, most legal representatives will implement the exchange of contracts by telephone, according to the Formulas provided by The Law Society[24]. This is done for speed and convenience. However, all the methods are discussed below and their strengths and weaknesses will be explained.

Each method will involve payment of the deposit for the purchase. The payment will usually take place either as a banker's draft or a solicitor's cheque. However, usually when there is a short period between exchange and completion, the legal representative of the seller can request from the legal representative of the buyer not to transfer the deposit money, and instead to "hold it to order". Essentially the deposit will not be transferred but instead be held by the legal firm representing the buyer in the name of the legal firm representing the seller. This will simplify the accounting entries that have to be made by the seller's legal representative and will also result in fewer telegraphic transfer fees. The legal representative of the buyer will hold the deposit, until the full purchase price is paid upon the completion of the transaction. It is important to note that if the buyer were to pull out of the sale at this stage, even though they would still be holding the deposit monies, they would be bound to transfer it to the seller's legal representative.

a.   EXCHANGE IN PERSON

As the name suggests, this method will involve the buyer's legal representative meeting with the seller's legal representative. They will physically exchange their clients' signed contracts. The buyer's legal representative will also provide the other legal representative with the buyer's means of funding the agreed deposit: either a banker's draft or a solicitor's cheque.

Subsequently, they will write in the agreed completion dates into each of the contracts and the date of the exchange. This method is arguably the safest method of implementing the exchange process because it is immediate and as both legal representatives can check that the contracts are identical.

However, this method is rarely used now a day because it requires both legal representatives to physically meet. As we have mentioned several times already, conveyancing is a time-sensitive process. Exchanging in person is practically inconvenient unless the two legal representatives are based nearby each other. Exchange in person is even more difficult for a chain of transactions, as the inconvenience of travelling to meet with more than one legal representative is greater.

b. EXCHANGE BY POST (OR DOCUMENT EXCHANGE)

Where exchange is implemented by post, the buyer's legal representative will post their client's signed contract, as well as a banker's draft or a solicitor's client account cheque for the agreed deposit, to the seller's legal representative. Upon receipt of the posted documents, the seller's legal representative will post their client's signed contract to the buyer's legal representative.

There can be some flexibility in the order of events. The seller's legal representative can be the one who initiates the process. Although a contract does not usually come into existence until the buyer has received the seller's contract, this is not the case when exchange is implemented by post: the contract comes into existing at the point where the seller posts his part of the contract to the buyer.

However, the postal rules relating to acceptance can be excluded by including provisions in the contract to that effect. If the postal rules have not been excluded, the contract will be deemed to have come into existence even if the buyer never received the contract due to it having been lost in the post.

c. EXCHANGE BY TELEPHONE

For the prospective buyer or seller, the most crucial difference between all these methods lies with the point at which the contract is deemed to come into existence. Although a telephone exchange will involve a physical exchange of the contracts following the telephone conversation, the exchange is not implemented by that physical exchange.

Rather, the contract is deemed to come into existence upon the legal representatives agreeing during the telephone conversation that the exchange has taken place. The dilemma that legal practitioners faced in the past was that one party could attempt to undermine or withdraw from the contract by disputing the contents of the telephone conversation. Moreover, neither party could verify in person that the other's contract incorporates all the agreed terms or even that the other party has signed the other contract.

As a countermeasure and to minimise any uncertainty, the Law Society has designated 3 approved formulas for exchanging contracts by telephone or fax: A, B and C.

Formula A is applicable when the legal representative holds a contract signed by both the buyer and the seller.

Formula B is applicable when legal representatives hold only a contract signed by their own client.

Formula C is used when the transaction is a part of a chain.

Professional undertakings play an especially important role in the process of telephone exchange. The legal representatives that do not fulfil the undertakings they have given face the danger of having disciplinary actions taken against them.

i)   Formula A

Formula A is used when one legal representative holds both signed parts of the contract. Those two parts are identical, with the exception that one part has the signature of the buyer and the other part has the signature of the seller. The legal representative will insert the agreed completion date in each part of the contract.

Expert's View

The solicitors mutually agree that exchange will take place from that moment and the solicitor holding both parts confirms that, as of that moment, he or she holds the part signed by his or her client(s) to the order of the other.

He or she undertakes to send on the same day their signed part of the contract to the other solicitor's office either by first class post or by hand delivery (where both solicitors are members of the Document Exchange network). If the solicitor holding both parts is the buyer's solicitor, they will undertake to do the same along with a banker's draft or solicitor's client account cheque for the agreed deposit, which is usually 10% of the purchase price.

After this exchange, the solicitors must also draft file memos, which will record:

1)   The names of the speaking practitioners,

2)   The date and time of the exchange,

3)   The formula used (including any variations),

4)   The date of completion,

5)   The amount of the deposit being paid.

Philip Li,
Solicitor-Partner

ii) Formula B

Formula B is the most widely used option for exchanging contracts over the telephone. Each legal representative will have the contract signed by his or her client. During the phone conversation, the legal representatives will confirm that the contracts are identical and correctly signed and will insert the date and time of completion. Then they will declare that the exchange is effective as of the telephone conversation, by undertaking that the part of the contract they hold is being held on the other's order.

As with Formula A, each legal representative will undertake to send the part of the contract in their possession to the opposing legal representative on the same (or next) day by mail or hand delivery. The buyer's legal representative will also send a banker's draft or the solicitor's client account cheque for the deposit.

As with Formula A, the legal representative must draft file memos recording the aforementioned details.

iii) Formula C

To reflect the needs of a link of related property transactions, Formula C is split into two parts and requires a larger number of professional undertakings. The key difference between it and Formula B is that in C the buyer's legal representative is waiting for a confirmation from the seller's legal representative in order to proceed with the transaction. Of course, in this situation, the seller is a buyer in a related transaction and will give that confirmation only after exchanging contracts to buy another property.

Expert's View
Part I:
Part I will consist of the solicitors agreeing:
1)   The time for exchange,

2) *The completion date, and*

3) *To whom the deposit is to be paid.*

Each solicitor then confirms that he or she holds one part of the contract in the agreed form signed by his or her client or, if there is more than one client, by all of them. Each solicitor undertakes to the other that:

1) *He or she will continue to hold that part of the contract until the time for exchange of contracts and the exchange formula used; and*

2) *If the seller's solicitor so notifies the buyer's solicitor by fax or telephone (whichever was previously agreed), they will both at that point comply with Part II of the formula.*

Part II:

In Part II, each solicitor undertakes to the other to hold the part of the contract in his or her possession to the other's order, so that the contracts are exchanged at that moment, and to despatch it to the other on the same day.

The buyer's solicitor will further undertake to the seller's solicitor to despatch on that day, or to arrange for the despatch on that day, a banker's draft or solicitor's client account cheque for the full deposit specified in the contract to the seller's solicitor and/or to another solicitor whom the seller's solicitor nominates to be held on Formula C terms.

Philip Li,
Solicitor-Partner

As with Formulae A and B, file memos must be made with regards to the conversations in Part I and II of Formula C. The

Part I memo should record:
1. The names of the speaking practitioners,
2. The date and time of the conversation,
3. The formula used (including any variations),
4. The specified time later in the day for exchange,
5. The name of the practitioner to whom the deposit is to be paid.

The Part II memo should record:
1. The request to exchange,
2. The time of exchange,
3. The identities of the speakers.

This whole process has to be implemented within a single day. If this is not accomplished, then the process has to be started from the beginning.

d. FAX & E-MAIL

While fax or e-mails may be used to initiate the Law Society's telephone exchange formulae, they may not be used independently as a method of exchanging contracts.

5. AFTER EXCHANGE

After the contracts have been exchanged, both the buyer and seller's legal representatives will contact their respective clients to inform them that the exchange has taken place and to confirm the agreed completion date. Shortly after exchange, the legal representatives will need to deal with a couple of matters discussed below.

a. THE BUYER
i) Insurance

If the buyer is relying on a mortgage, it is likely that one of the conditions required by the lender will have been to acquire building insurance. In this case, the lender may have arranged the particulars relating to the insurance and the policy will activate automatically once exchange takes place.

Nonetheless, the buyer's legal representative should check to ensure that either contacting the lender or the insurers directly have activated the insurance policy.

ii) Registration

The buyer's legal representative may seek to protect the buyer's interest in the property (the sale) through registering it via a Notice at the Land Registry. This is advisable when there is a long delay between the exchange and completion and the buyer is concerned that the seller might be negotiating with another party. An interest can be recorded on the title registry by submitting a unilateral or agreed notice to the Land Registry. If the buyer has the consent of the seller to register the sale, then the notice will be agreed. If the buyer does not have the consent of the seller, then the notice is unilateral.

The effect of these Notices is to alert anyone who will consult the title registry that a sale of the property is in process. It will also notify the beneficiaries of the notice if another disposition is entered in the title registry. A notice can also be used to protect priority of interest, which cannot itself be registered or which is pending registration (if delayed). Both types of notice have the same fee, which you can find through the Land Registry's Website[39]. It is important to note that entering a notice will not protect the sale as such, as it does not stop other parties from entering their own restrictions or notices. In practice however, most legal representatives will not proceed with a transaction on a property, which has a notice of a contract for sale registered on the title registry of the property.

Standard practice is to register a sale with a notice if any of the below conditions are met:

» A dispute arises between parties

» Buyer feels that the seller is seeking to dispose of the property to someone else
» There is a long wait between exchange and completion.
» Seller delays completion
» Purchase price is to be paid in instalments – the purchase deed to be executed after payment of the final instalment.

b.   THE SELLER
i)   Existing Mortgage

If the seller's property has a mortgage, their legal representative has to write to the lender in order to request a mortgage redemption statement for their client's mortgage (its outstanding balance) calculated to the date of completion. It is only possible to obtain an accurate redemption figure for the seller's mortgage after an agreed completion date has been established.

With this redemption statement, the seller's legal representative should also request the lender to include a daily rate of interest in case delays cause the completion date to be revised. This is in preparation for when the seller actually receives the buyer's monies, after which the seller can pay the redemption figure.

CHAPTER SIX
Pre-Completion

Once contracts have been exchanged and the steps required immediately after exchange have been taken care of, it is time to begin preparations for the completion of the transaction. In some transactions, the exchange and completion are simultaneous, which requires all the steps that are described in this chapter to be completed before the exchange of contracts.

It is important for the buyer to have communicated his intentions to exchange and complete on the same day to his legal representative when giving the initial instructions. The timing of a simultaneous exchange and completion requires substantial planning and must be established well in advance of the action day of exchange and completion.

This is even more important when the buyer is relying on a mortgage, as the lender will need time to go over all of the pre-completion documents. In many cases lenders will ask for a minimum period of over a week to review the pre-completion documents in which case it is crucial that the following steps be done well before exchange of contracts in order to not delay the completion.

First, in order to establish what steps are necessary before completion, first we need to have a clear understanding of what completion is.

1. MEANING OF COMPLETION

When the contracts were exchanged, you will recall that the buyer's legal representative will have provided the seller's legal representative with the deposit for the purchase, either in the form of a banker's draft, a solicitor's client account cheque or by "holding it to order". 'Completion' is the point at which the remainder of the purchase price is transferred over to the seller, after which the transaction will be 'completed'.

This will usually involve the lender releasing the remainder of the mortgage funds to the buyer (if applicable), who will then transfer it to the seller. Both parties will, in most cases, agree upon having a certain amount of time between exchange and completion in order to ensure that all matters relating to completion are in order.

2. THE TRANSFER DEED

a. FORMALITIES

A transfer of property from one person to another must be made by deed for it to be legally valid. By 'deed', we are referring to a document that has been executed in accordance with formalities required by law to guarantee that its validity.

For modern conveyancing, a deed must:

a) Make it clear on the face of the document that it is intended to be a deed:

b) Be signed by the person executing the deed in the presence of a witness who attests the signature; and

c) Be delivered by the person executing it or by someone authorised to do so on his or her behalf.

For a witness to 'attest' the signature, they must watch as the deed is signed by the people executing it and then they must themselves sign the deed to declare that they witnessed this event. Any individual can be a witness, however obtaining an independent witness is recommended in all circumstances. If there are unforeseen complications and the validity of the document is called into question, an independent witness may benefit you.

A deed takes effect on delivery. In the past, 'delivered' referred to the moment where one party physically handed over the document. However, for the purposes of modern property transactions, the crucial element is that the person executing the deed must have indicated in some way that they intended to be bound by the deed. This is often satisfied by the inclusion of a clause in the deed that specifies the time on which the deed is delivered (e.g. after completion).

The above formalities must be strictly adhered to. While a failure to do so may not necessarily cause the ultimate failure of your conveyance, it will undoubtedly cause further costs and delay in the process.

b. PREPARING THE TRANSFER DEED

Preparing the draft Transfer Deed is usually the responsibility of the buyer's legal representative, although the seller's legal representative may be inclined to prepare the first draft in certain circumstances, (i.e. in respect of sales of part or sales of multiple properties by a single individual).

When the buyer's legal representative has prepared the draft transfer deed, they should send it to the seller's legal representative, who will check it to confirm that its contents correspond with the contract's provisions. Amendments may be suggested and the draft may have to be returned.

Once the seller's legal representative approves the draft transfer deed and any amendments have been agreed upon, the buyer's legal representative would traditionally prepare an engrossment of the transfer deed. This is essentially an elaborate term for the final version of a legal document typed on special paper. However, the buyer should discuss the matter of engrossment with its legal representative in advance and ensure there are no additional fees. Paying for a special paper version of the transfer deed might not be justified, considering that the document will invariably be scanned by the Land Registry and stored electronically.

In respect of registered land, transfer deeds must be written on forms provided by the Land Registry: If you are transferring the whole of an existing registered title, then your legal representatives will have to use Form TR1[25]. If you are selling only a part of your property (i.e. you are selling your garden to the neighbour), then the correct form will be TP1[26].

The exact content of those forms should be communicated and confirmed before the completion takes place. We will discuss the completion process in more detail in the next chapter, however once the transfer of the outstanding funds has been confirmed, the seller's legal representative will send the buyer's legal representative the relevant form (TR1[25] or TP1[26]), executed as a deed. Then the buyer's legal representative will send the form to the Land Registry, along with other documents, to register the transfer.

3. REQUISITIONS ON TITLE & REPLIES

As discussed in earlier chapters, it may be that the contract prevents requisitions from being made after exchange has taken place. However, it is traditional for requisitions on title to be made at this stage of the conveyancing process. Please refer to the previous section for more details.

If pre-completion requisitions are made at this stage, the parties should be mindful of the deadline – completion of the sale. If the exchange and completion take place on the same day, then those pre-completion requisitions should have been raised before the exchange. At this stage, the requisitions relate mainly to the logistics of the move (i.e. moving date, exchange of keys). Provided the buyer's legal representative is satisfied with those replies, the next step would be to execute (in other words sign) the transfer deed by going through the formalities previously discussed.

The seller must always execute the Transfer Deed as they are transferring their ownership of the property, whereas the buyer will only need to execute the Transfer Deed if it contains a covenant.

4. MORTGAGE DEED AND MORTGAGE REDEMPTION STATEMENT

It is at this stage that the buyer should execute a mortgage deed if they are relying on a mortgage to buy their property. The mortgage deed will be drawn up by the lender, and serves to protect the lender's interest in the property. It will reflect the contents of the mortgage offer, discussed in Chapter 4, specifying the general and special (where they apply) conditions.

If they have not done so already and the seller's property is mortgaged, the seller's legal representative should request a mortgage redemption statement from their client's lender, as discussed in Chapter 5.

5. STAMP DUTY LAND TAX (SDLT) RETURN

Stamp Duty Land Tax (SDLT) is a tax on property transactions over a certain threshold in England, Wales and Northern Ireland. Currently, the threshold is of £125,000 for residential properties. The purchaser is responsible for paying SDLT and submitting the associated return form. For some property transactions, such as a charity purchasing a property or local authorities making a compulsory purchase order, you may apply for relief or exemption from paying SDLT and filing a return.

Payment of SDLT and the submission of the return form are normally done online by the buyer's legal representative. As a non-legal professional, the only way to pay your SDLT liability is by submitting a form which would have to be filled out and sent to the HM Revenue and Customs along with the payment. However, this should only be necessary in the case where you have not instructed a legal representative in the purchase of your property. We will discuss the forms to fill out later in the chapter.

The SDLT must be submitted within 30 days of the date when the charge to tax arises, or the 'effective date', as late payments may incur interest and/or penalties. The date when the tax arises will normally be the date of completion, although this may arise earlier depending on the situation. For example, where:

»   The buyer has provided at least 90% of the purchase price, or
»   The buyer has the right to occupy the land, or
»   The buyer has the right to receive rents, or
»   The buyer has paid rent.

a.   RATES OF SDLT

Below is a table with the latest set of Stamp Duty Land Taxes, which became effective on 4th December 2014:

On/After 4th December 2014:

Price of property ≤ £125,000	0%
£125,000 < Price ≤ £250,000	2%
£250,000 < Price ≤ £925,000	5%
£925,000 < Price ≤ £1,500,000	10%
For the remainder (if any)	12%

The amount of tax owed is calculated cumulatively. If this is your first property, there will not be any SDLT owed where the net value of the property is £125,000 or less, although an SDLT return must nonetheless be filed.

If for example the net value of the property is £450,000, the amount of SDLT owed will be the following:

0% on the first £125,000 =	£0
2% on the next £125,000 =	£2,500
5% on the remainder of £200,000 =	£10,000
This results in a total SDLT obligation of:	£12,500

These rates are not the only variables to consider when calculating SDLT owed from your property transaction. The calculation of SDLT is dependent on various factors, such as the number and value of fixtures belonging to the land, whether the property is leasehold or whether the property transaction is linked. You should refer to the government calculator tool[27] for a more accurate SDLT quote.

b. HIGHER RATE TRANSACTIONS

Since 1st April 2016, there is a higher rate of SDLT for owning additional homes. HMRC guidance indicates that owning a property outside of the UK, or anywhere in the world, will mean that you already own a property for the purposes of the additional property SDLT liability. A 3% SDLT surcharge will be added to the standard rates listed above. This surcharge applies to acquisitions of a major interest in an additional dwelling for £40,000 or more in England, Wales and Northern Ireland. In short, it applies to additional residential homes or buy-to-let properties that are bought for £40,000 or more.

A 'major interest' is the freehold or a lease for a term of more than 7 years. Caravans, mobile homes, houseboats and garden land sold separately from a dwelling are excluded from the definition of 'a dwelling', however holiday homes are included for the purposes of SDLT. If the second property is replacing your main residence, which you have already sold, then there will be no 3% surcharge.

If you have not sold your main residence at the time of purchase, you will be liable for paying the extra 3%. However, if you sell your old property within the next 36 months, you can apply for a refund of the additional SDLT paid. You should consult your legal representatives and/or an accountant for further information on the process.

On/After 1st April 2016:

Price of property ≤ £125,000	3%
£125,000 < Price ≤ £250,000	5%
£250,000 < Price ≤ £925,000	8%
£925,000 < Price ≤ £1,500,000	13%
For the remainder (if any)	15%

For example, where the net value of the property being bought is £550,000, the amount of SDLT owed for this 'higher rate transaction' will be:

3% on the first £125,000 =	£3,750
5% on the next £125,000 =	£6,250
8% on the remainder of £300,000 =	£24,000
This results in a total SDLT obligation of:	£34,000

It is also worth noting that the higher rate will apply where the buyer owns additional properties situated outside England, Wales or Northern Ireland.

c. LEASES

For transactions involving new leases, it is important to remember that calculations relating to the duty on a premium and on the lease rent are done separately. For example, a developer builds a new property and sells it on a 125-year lease. The sale price is £400,000 and the rent for the lease is £5,000 per year. You will calculate the SDLT payable on the premium of £400,000 in the standard way described above.

Assuming it is your only property, it will be:

0% on the first £125,000 =	£0
2% on the next £125,000 =	£2,500
5% on the remainder of £150,000 =	£7,500
This results in a total SDLT obligation of:	£10,000

Because this is a new residential lease that includes paying actual rent (as opposed to a symbolic rent payment), you will have to calculate the Net present value of the £5,000 rent payment over the 125 years of the lease.

Once again, the calculator[27] provided by HMRC will be a good guide for establishing the net present value of all future annual rent payments. If the net present value is above £125,000, then the portion that exceeds this threshold will be taxed at 1%. This will be in addition to the £10,000 SDLT payable on the premium of the property.

The above calculation for SDLT on rent is not applicable in the case the lease is for less than 7 years and in the case of an assignment of an old lease (for example: buying the lease when there are 100 years left of the 125-year lease).

If a legal representative is dealing with your property sale/purchase, it would be their responsibility to ensure that the correct SDLT is paid. If you are not instructing a legal representative, given the complex nature of SDLT, it may be advisable to seek the professional help of an accountant or legal representative to ensure that you pay the correct SDLT.

d. SDLT RETURN FORMS

Some of the HMRC's online services[28], such as submitting an SDLT return are only available to law firms or other such companies. Filling out the SDLT return online is guaranteed to be the fastest and most secure method of completing the transaction. However, your legal representative needs to be registered to the HMRC's online services.

Otherwise, physical forms will need to be ordered, which might slow down the payment. The forms may be ordered both online and over the phone and HMRC will try to deliver the forms to you within 2 weeks. For this reason, it is crucial that these forms are ordered before completion.

There are a number of forms used to submit SDLT returns:

i)   SDLT1

This is the standard form that needs to be completed for the payment of SDLT and it will be sufficient for straightforward transactions. The form includes a payslip. The government provides a helpful guide[29] to assist people in the filling out of the form.

ii)   SDLT2

If there are 2 or more buyers or sellers, then the form SDLT2 will need to be filled out, alongside SDLT1. It will list the details of all the additional parties in the transaction.

iii)   SDLT3

When the transaction involves more than one property, the form SDLT3 should be included with the form SDLT1. SDLT3 should be filled out for each additional property purchased.

iv)   SDLT4

Use the form SDLT4 in conjunction with SDLT1, if any of the following conditions apply:

1. the sale of the property is part of a business sale;
2. the buyer is a company;
3. when any part of the consideration is uncertain;
4. when you have asked HMRC for guidance on application;
5. when there are deferment provision arrangements with HMRC;
6. when there are mineral rights reserved.

v)   SDLT16

This is a refund form in case the higher SDLT rate is no longer payable, because the first property was sold within 36 months of the purchase of the second property. It can be completed either online or in postal form, with more guidance on the format and methods on the government website[30].

Once HMRC has received and approved your SDLT payment and return, they will issue your legal representative with an SDLT5 certificate, which confirms receipt of the return. This certificate must be sent later to the Land Registry, alongside your application for registration.

6. PRE-COMPLETION SEARCHES

As the name suggests, pre-completion searches are normally implemented after contracts have been exchanged and before completion of the transaction. Carrying out pre-completion searches is usually the responsibility of the buyer's legal representative, which is understandable as it is the buyer who may stand to be affected by the results of such searches.

You will recall from earlier chapters that the principle of caveat emptor is still applicable to property transactions, which means that the buyer is responsible for checking the suitability of his purchase. Pre-completion searches are a means for the buyer's legal representative to fulfil that responsibility by verifying that the information obtained at the pre-exchange stage remains unchanged.

In addition to the traditional pre-completion searches, a buyer's legal representative might carry out searches to supplement those effected at the pre-exchange stage, perhaps due to a lack of time as a result of the parties wanting a speedy exchange or in order to verify information provided after the exchange of contracts.

Pre-completion searches may also represent a means of fulfilling a responsibility owed to another party: the lender. Where the buyer is relying on a mortgage for their purchase, the buyer's legal representative must also carry out these searches in order to protect the lender's interest by ensuring that adverse or additional entries have not been made against the title since the exchange of contracts.

Expert's View

It is important that the results of any pre-completion searches, carried out by the buyer's solicitor, are received early so that there is adequate time between the point at which the buyer's solicitor is in receipt of 'clear' search results and the date of completion. Otherwise, there will not be sufficient time to resolve any matters that may be revealed in the search results.

If there is a long period between exchange and completion, it is advisable to order the searches between 5-7 working days prior to the date of completion. Conversely, the buyer's solicitor should perhaps arrange to have the searches begun, either immediately upon their client signing the contract or earlier than the recommended 5-7 working days, where delays in the receipt of replies is anticipated e.g. through industrial action.

All of the pre-completion searches can be completed online. A buyer's solicitor should have access to the HM Land Registry online portal called 'Land Registry Direct'. Some case management systems also now integrate the Land Registry search facility.

HMLR is shifting away from paper applications and all searches to the Land Registry can now be made online. Further, a paper application takes longer to process and costs more so your solicitor

should generally be making online applications.
Cindi Van Graan,
Sole-Practitioner Solicitor

There are primarily 3 searches that are traditionally carried out at the pre-completion stage. These are:
a)   Land Registry Official Search;
b)   Land Charges Department Search;
c)   Companies Search.

a.   LAND REGISTRY OFFICIAL SEARCH

The search can be conducted against the whole of the registered title or against a part of it, using the forms OS1[31] and OS2[32], respectively. The purpose of the search is to confirm that no adverse entries or pending applications have been made against the title after the 'search from date', which should be the date when the initial copies of the register of title were ordered.

Importantly, an official search of a whole of a title can be ordered with priority. This will give the party that ordered the search a 30 business-day priority period, during which no other party can register any adverse interests over the property. If the transaction involves a lender, the search must be made in the name of the lender, for the lender to receive the 30-day protection and be able to register the mortgage.

b.   LAND CHARGES DEPARTMENT SEARCH

Search applications to the Land Charges Department are important for unregistered land and for bankruptcy searches. There are two main forms that are used for those searches: K15 is used for unregistered land and K16 is used for a bankruptcy search. The fees for these searches are currently of £2 per name searched.

The legal representative of the buyer needs to obtain a clear bankruptcy search before the lenders can release the mortgage funds. This bankruptcy search will investigate whether the buyer has any debts, or is bankrupt. The K16[33] bankruptcy search can have two outcomes: either there are no subsisting entries (the search results will be on form K17) or there will be entries revealed (the search results will be on form K18).

Expert's View

By way of an example, I applied for a bankruptcy search two days before the expected exchange date, and an adverse entry was revealed which related to an unpaid loan, which my client knew absolutely nothing about. After reviewing the official copy I obtained by submitting a K19 application form, I was able to investigate further and make relevant phone calls the supposed creditor to have the entry removed.

Another way of dealing with an adverse entry is for the client to swear a Statutory Declaration, which confirms the entry does not relate to them in any way and that they are not subject to any actual or impending insolvency proceedings. The buyer's solicitor will draft this and ask the buyer to swear it at a different solicitor's firm, which is independent of the transaction. It is not uncommon for an entry to be revealed if you have a common name for instance.

Cindi Van Graan,
Sole-Practitioner Solicitor

In case the results indicate entries in the bankruptcy index, the buyer's legal representative can apply for the official copy of the bankruptcy entry, using form K19[34]. In this later case, it is important for the buyer's solicitors to take action in order for the sale to continue.

c. COMPANIES SEARCH

If the buyer or seller is a company, it becomes important to conduct a search with the government's Companies House. This will confirm whether the company is undergoing insolvency proceedings or whether it was struck off the register of companies.

There is a small fee for the search (£7 for postal and £3 for online search). Online search are more expedient, with the results becoming available instantly. Company House's online services are only available to companies with a Land registry online account, however they can also be ordered through search agencies such as iCompile Searches.

Companies House Beta[35] is the .Gov website that is open to the public to carry out online searches and company documents can be accessed instantly online in PDF format. The acting legal representative may have a Companies House Direct subscription, which will give them instant access to a wider range of documents, which can be obtained, for a fee of £1 each.

7. COMPLETION STATEMENT AND FINANCIAL STATEMENT

The seller's legal representative should provide the buyer's legal representative with a Completion statement that lists several different financial details. The Completion statement will list the purchase price for the property, apportionment for outgoings and price paid for chattels like furniture and appliances. The statement will add those and list the final amount payable to the seller.

The apportionment will depend on the type of property and are more frequent for leasehold properties. Often the owner selling the leasehold interest will have paid the annual ground rent, and will require the buyer to pay for a portion of it, based on the completion date.

For example, if the ground rent is £1,000 for the year 1st February 2017 – 31st January 2018 and was paid on 1st February 2017, then a buyer completing on 31st July can expect a £500 ground rent charge in the Completion statement to reflect 6 months of ownership. A few different charges can be apportioned, like water, electricity and gas.

Conversely, if the expense is incurred by the seller, and will later be paid by the buyer (i.e. the ground rent in the above example for 1st February 2017 – 31st January 2018 year will be payable on 31st January 2018), then the apportionment will decrease the overall price the buyer needs to pay. If the leasehold is subject to a tenancy, the rent paid by the tenant will be apportioned too, leading, again, to a reduction of the completion sum.

The outgoings can be apportioned in the sale of a freehold too. However, the apportionment of any council tax paid will not be in the Completion statement, and instead will be done by the local council.

The Standard Conditions of Sale stipulate that the property belongs to the seller until the end of the completion day, which means that all apportionment periods starts from the day after completion. Furthermore, sometimes it is not possible to give an accurate amount of the expenses incurred by the seller for the period up to completion. As a result, an estimate is made that is subject to later revisions.

Sometimes the seller's legal representative will retain a portion of the sale proceeds for a period from 6 to 12 months after completion. That money can be paid to the buyer, in case the expenses apportioned exceed the estimates made in the Completion Statement.

Additionally, the lender's legal representative will also send a Completion statement to the buyer's legal representative. It will contain the mortgage amount and several fees that will be subtracted from the loan: e.g. administration fees, Land Registry fees, OS1[31] and K16[33] searches fees, telegraphic transfer fees. The statement presents the balance after subtracting all those expenses from the mortgage amount.

Once the buyer's legal representative has received the Completion Statements from the seller and the lender, they will prepare a Financial Statement. It will contain all the information from the Completion Statement of the seller (purchase price plus different expenses) and the Completion statement of the lender (mortgage amount minus different fees). The Financial Statement will also include the professional fees and expenses of the legal representative of the buyer: e.g. search fees, legal representative's fees, fees for transfer to seller's legal representative, etcetera. The Financial Statement will present the final amount that the buyer needs to transfer to his legal representative in order for completion to take place.

Similarly, the seller's legal representative will add to the Completion Statement they send to the buyer's legal representative all their professional fees and expenses in a Financial Statement to the seller. The statement might also include an estate agent commission, a mortgage redemption fee and a number of other possible expenses incurred in the process of sale. This statement will give the seller the exact amount of proceeds that will be transferred to him at completion.

Of course, you should inquire with your legal representative if you are uncertain about some charges or if you believe you have paid for them already.

8. ANCILLARY MATTERS

a. OCCUPATION PRIOR TO COMPLETION

The buyer might express a desire to move in before the completion of the transaction if they have already sold off their old property. Allowing this is an important decision with serious consequences for the seller.

Expert's View

Generally, I would advise against this. The seller will want to avoid granting the buyer a right of possession without having completed the transaction and being in receipt of the full purchase monies.

If the parties do agree access prior to completion, it should only be granted under a Licence to Occupy. This ensures that the buyer has no right of possession and that no relationship of landlord and tenant is created, so that if for some reason completion does not take place then the Buyer will have to vacate the property.

A buyer should also bear in mind that access to the property before completion may be viewed as the 'effective date of completion' for SDLT purposes and the SDLT liability then becomes due from that point.

If a buyer just wants access to make measurements for decoration or building works then access should be arranged via a 'Key Undertaking'. This will allow the buyer access to the property to undertake those works but only on the agreement that if the buyer causes damage to the property he will compensate (indemnify) the seller against all losses. Access should be agreed once contracts have been exchanged, and only for access and not for actual occupation of the property.

Cindi Van Graan,
Sole-Practitioner Solicitor

b.   INSURANCE PRIOR TO COMPLETION

When selling a leasehold property, the owner of the freehold will be responsible for maintaining insurance over the building. It is important for the buyer's legal representative to see a copy of the insurance policy before completion.

When selling a freehold property, the buyer will be responsible for ensuring the property is covered by insurance. As we discussed in the previous chapters, the insurance coverage should start from the exchange of contracts. While this is strongly recommended in any transaction, the lender in transactions involving a mortgage will likely require it. It is possible to amend the default position and make the seller responsible for insurance coverage between exchange of contracts and completion. Special Conditions need to be included in the contract to affect such a change and amend the Standard Conditions of Sale, which place the responsibility on the buyer.

It is important for the buyer to have insurance over the property, because even if there is an accident and the property is destroyed, he will still be required to complete the purchase. It should be noted, that if the seller has a mortgage, then it is likely that he is required to have insurance over the property.

If a buyer purchases insurance coverage starting from exchange, then he will not be able to cover accidental damage of the property, because he is not in occupation. Once the purchase is completed and the buyer becomes in occupation, he should contact the insurer and amend the policy to cover accidental damage.

Once the sale is completed, the seller can proceed to cancel his insurance on the property. He will most likely not be able to do this before completion, as mortgage lenders usually require the borrower to have insurance over the property at all times. Only after the mortgage has been discharged will the borrower be able to cancel the insurance over the property. Otherwise, he will be in violation of the mortgage terms.

The buyer will have to consider purchasing life insurance too. It is common for lenders to require borrowers to purchase life insurance, for them to have some security of repayment. The death of the borrower will be a truly tragic event from a personal perspective, however it will also mean a default from the perspective of the lender and all lenders seek to ensure their capital is secure.

c. FINANCIAL MATTERS

The buyer should confirm with the lender when the mortgage funds will be released. This should happen before the completion date.

Sometimes a lender will release funds before the completion date and will hold the buyer responsible for paying interest on the funds for the period from release to completion. Waiting for the mortgage funds to be released on completion day can cause a lot of emotional drain on the buyer, as he is waiting in uncertainty until the last minute. As a result, receiving the funds early might be beneficial.

Your legal representative can contact the bank and request the funds. The bank should be aware of the completion date and will use that as a guide when releasing the funds. You can contact them to discuss the exact date of release. Furthermore, your legal representative should account to you for any interest the money has accrued over the period from receiving the funds to the completion of the transaction.

It should also be noted that different payment methods take

different times. If the lender releases the funds through CHAPS, then the payment will take place on the same day. However, if the lender sends a cheque, then it might take 5 days for the payment to be cleared.

In case the lender does not provide the money on time for completion, then the buyer will have to pay interest on the outstanding amount to the seller, as agreed in the contract. The Law Society's contract rate, which can be found in the Standard Conditions of Sale, is 4% above the current Barclays Bank base rate. As of March 2017, the Barclays Bank base rate is 0.5%, which means you will have to pay an annual interest of 4.5%, based on the amount outstanding to the seller and the number of days the payment is in arrears.

9.   CERTIFICATE OF TITLE

Usually, about one week before completion is scheduled to take place, the buyer's legal representative will send the lender the Certificate of Title. We already discussed this document in the preceding chapters. A Report on Title was sent to both the buyer and the lender after all the searches were conducted. However, lenders require different packages of documents at different stages of the conveyancing process.

As we discussed above, a number of additional searches were conducted as part of the Pre-completion process. Those included a full priority search, bankruptcy search and land charges search, to name a few. While this practice will differ from lender to lender, the results obtained for most of the searches described in this chapter will have to be sent to the lender as part of the Pre-completion procedure. The lender will send the buyer's legal representative a detailed list of the different documents that need to be submitted in the stages of the transaction.

Several different undertakings will have to be made by your legal representative too. A few examples are: a Fund Request, which will officially request the mortgage advance to be transferred on a specific date; a SDLT 1 Form undertaking, which is a promise by the buyer's legal representative to submit the relevant Stamp Duty Land Tax forms; a Pre-completion Undertaking (form TA13[18]), which contains a promise by the seller's legal representative that the sale proceeds will be used to discharge any existing mortgage over the property.

An important element of the package is the form AP1[36], which will be sent to the Land Registry in order to register the transfer. The form describes different elements of the transfer and will have to be filled out by the buyer's legal representative. It will then have to be signed by the lender, in case the buyer is using a mortgage. Usually, the filled-out form will be provided to the lender with the other Pre-completion searches to facilitate the completion process.

CHAPTER SEVEN
Ready for Completion and Post-Completion

As mentioned previously, completion is the point at which the buyer pays the remainder of the purchase price to the seller. In response, the seller's legal representatives will provide the buyer's legal representatives with the executed Transfer Deed, vacant possession (provided that this was included in the contract), and instruct the estate agent to release the keys to the buyer. If the seller's property is unregistered, they will also give the buyer their title deeds, however as previously mentioned now a day it is rare for a property to be unregistered.

It is important to note that is not the end. After completion, ownership of the property will only transfer to the buyer once they have been registered as the registered proprietor of the property at the Land Registry.

1. THE DATE OF COMPLETION

As you may recall, the completion date will have been agreed upon when the contracts were exchanged. It is standard practice for completion to occur 7 to 28 days after contracts have been exchanged and the time of completion is usually agreed as 1pm or 2pm. This is to afford the seller's legal representative with sufficient time to redeem any mortgage over the property and to send the sale proceeds to the seller.

It is possible for completion to occur on the same day as exchange. By doing so, the parties have the benefit of facilitating a faster conveyance and a deposit is unnecessary, as the entire purchase price would be provided at the same time. However, whether this remains a viable course of action will depend on various factors:

» If your property transaction has related sales involved, the risk of something going wrong will rise proportionate to the number of links in the property chain. Moreover, transactions involving chains must be completed on the same day.

» If you are buying and relying on a mortgage, it might be impractical to have the exchange on the same day as the completion as the lender may take some time to release the mortgage funds. Then again, this could be remedied by ensuring that the mortgage funds are released the day before.

» Furthermore, some lenders require a minimum period of time between exchange and completion.

The seller's legal representative will confirm to the buyer's legal representative that completion has taken place once the former is in receipt of the full purchase monies from the latter. Subsequently, the seller's legal representative will release the keys to the estate agent and confirm to the buyer's legal representative that they have done so.

2. ELEMENTS OF COMPLETION

a. REQUISITIONS

The buyer's legal representative has raised requisitions on numerous occasions by this stage of the process, as we have explained in the preceding chapters. One last set of questions that he raises come in the form of the TA13[18] form, completion information and undertakings (2nd edition). This form usually

119

must be included in the package of documents that has to be sent to the lender as part of their Pre-completion checks. This document bundle was discussed in the end of the previous chapter.

This form allows the seller's legal representative to specify the firm's bank details and a method of completion. If completion by post is chosen, he can undertake to use the Law Society's Code of Completion by Post. Furthermore, the seller's legal representative can undertake to discharge any existing mortgage. Those undertakings are taken very seriously and violating them can lead to disciplinary actions against the legal representative. The form also contains questions about vacant possession and collection of the keys.

b.   NOTICE OF ASSIGNMENT

When the property being sold is leasehold, the lease needs to be assigned. In order to complete the transaction, a Notice of Assignment must be served on the holder of the freehold interest. Until such a notice is served, the seller will be liable for any breach of covenant (e.g. maintenance and allowed use) and any financial obligations (e.g. ground rent and service charges).

Normally, a provision in the original lease describe the process of giving the Notice of Assignment, with the buyer's legal representative being most often the party responsible for submitting the notice.

c.   DEED OF COVENANT

A Deed of Covenant is used to protect the interests of the assignee of the lease: the buyer of the leasehold estate as well as the Managing Company of the property. They are an important tripartite contract that ensures the buyer will have the benefit and burden of the covenants and will be able to exercise his rights against any management company that might be servicing the property. Privity of estate allows the buyer to sue the landlord for any breaches of the covenants, however it does not grant an express right to the buyer to sue the management company. The Landlord and Tenant (Covenants) Act 1995[37] does clarify the legal position with regards to the relationship between tenant and management company and as a result Deeds of Covenant are not a legal necessity anymore.

Nevertheless, a lot of lease agreements will require such a covenant to be executed. Usually, the seller's legal representative will provide the buyer's legal representative with the required form. Then the buyer will have to execute the document as a deed. This will create a direct contractual relationship between the buyer and the landlord/management company.

d.   MORTGAGE ADVANCE

We already discussed different complications that arise from receiving the mortgage advance too early in the previous chapter. However, it is important to emphasize that the legal representative of the buyer should specifically request for the mortgage advance to be sent in the week before the completion takes place.

> **Expert's View**
>
> *The buyer's solicitor will submit a Certificate of Title to the mortgage lender approximately 7 working days before the date of completion. This 'Certificate of Title' is the solicitor's report on title to the lender and is also the request for the mortgage advance to be released to the solicitor's client account.*
>
> *A buyer's solicitor will want to receive the mortgage funds the working day before the completion date set in the contract. It is unwise to request funds to arrive on the day set for completion because the bank utilises a CHAPs same day*

payment which only guarantees to arrive by 4.30pm.
This of course means that if the funds arrive at
4.30pm on the day of completion it will be too late
to complete.

Cindi Van Graan,
Sole-Practitioner Solicitor

e. MORTGAGE REDEMPTION STATEMENT

The seller's legal representative should contact the lender of the
seller and request a mortgage redemption statement. This
statement will show the exact amount that needs to be repaid on
the mortgage and should also show any redemption fees that
would be applicable. Banks charge these fees as compensation
for any interest profits that would-be loss if the mortgage is
redeemed earlier than scheduled. Different lenders charge
different fees, with early redemptions costing the borrower
anywhere between interest payments for one month to interest
payment for 12 month.

f. CONFIRMATIONS

Several phone calls will take place throughout the day of
completion. The buyer's legal representative will enquire whether
the legal representative of the seller has the completed TR1[25] form
(which was discussed in the previous chapter) and insure it is
ready to be mailed. He will also confirm the outstanding amount
that needs to be transferred for completion to take place.

Once the seller's legal representative receives the
outstanding amount from the buyer's legal representative, he
needs to inform him that the transfer was received and the
purchase completed. Then he can inform the estate agent to
release the keys to the property to the buyer. He will also inform
the seller that the transaction was completed and will prepare for

the advance of the outstanding sale proceeds to be transferred to the seller.

The buyer's legal representative will inform the buyer that the purchase was completed, once he receives the confirmation from the legal representative of the seller.

Then the two legal representatives can start attending to post-completion matters, which will be discussed later.

3.   CHAIN OF TRANSACTIONS

When the sale is a part of a chain of related transactions, the process of completion is complicated significantly. It is very important for all the transfer of funds to be completed as soon as practically possible, in order to finish the full chain of transactions on the agreed completion date.

Expert's View

Where there is a chain of transactions, it is necessary for the buyer's solicitor at the bottom of the chain to send their funds first so that the seller's solicitor will have sufficient funds for the seller's related purchase. And all this needs to be done in good time to ensure completion takes place by the time stated in the contract (1pm or 2pm).

It is also important for all parties in the chain to send their funds as soon as practicable so as to ensure that any onward bank transfers for mortgage redemptions are completed on the day of completion. Most banks have a same day CHAPs payment deadline of 3.30 pm to ensure funds clear on the same day.

Cindi Van Graan,
Sole-Practitioner Solicitor

Here is a sample order of activities that will take a place in a transaction that involves three parties: Person 1 buying from Person 2, who is buying from Person 3. The example will assume that the purchases involve mortgage lending and estate agents.

a. PERSON 1 BUYING PROPERTY A

The legal representative of Person 1 should receive the mortgage advance for Property A before the completion, on the date specified in the request for mortgage advance that was included with the Certificate on Title send to the lender (described earlier in this chapter).

Once the legal representative has the funds, he should send the outstanding amount (i.e. full purchase price minus the paid deposit) to the legal representative of Person 2.

Once he received confirmation from the legal representative of Person 2, he can inform Person 1 that the purchase was completed and can start attending to post-completion matters.

b. PERSON 2 SELLING PROPERTY A AND BUYING PROPERTY B

Similarly, the legal representative of Person 2 should also receive the mortgage advance for Property B before completion.

Once the legal representative of Person 2 receives the purchase funds from the legal representative of Person 1, he will confirm the completion to him and will inform the estate agent to release the keys to Person 1. Then the legal representative will confirm to his client (Person 2) that the sale of Property A is completed.

Then the legal representative of Person 2 would proceed to pay the outstanding amount for the purchase of Property B to the legal representative of Person 3. For the purpose, he will use the mortgage funds received for Property B and any balance from the sale proceeds of Property A that is not needed for the redemption of the mortgage over Property A and the payment to the estate agents. Once he receives confirmation of the payment from the legal representative of Person 3, he can inform his client (Person 2) that the purchase of Property B is completed.

Then the legal representative of Person 2 can redeem the mortgage over Property A and pay the estate agents that marketed Property A. After this he will be able to attend to the post-completion matters.

c.   PERSON 3 SELLING PROPERTY B

When the legal representative of Person 3 receives the purchase funds from the legal representative of Person 2, he will confirm the completion to him and will inform the estate agent to release the keys to Person 2. Then the legal representative will confirm to his client (Person 3) that the sale of Property B is completed.

Then the legal representative of Person 3 can redeem the mortgage over Property B and pay the estate agents that marketed Property B. He will pay the outstanding sale proceeds to Person 3 and subsequently attend the post-completion matters.

4.   FAILURE TO COMPLETE

It is the seller's legal representative that confirms that completion has taken place. Even after the buyer's legal representative has sent the funds, the other side must confirm the funds were received. Only then will they arrange for the keys to be released and passed on.

If for some reason the buyer's legal representative does not make the payment (e.g. the funds are not released, or the buyer has changed his mind), then the seller can serve a notice to complete on the buyer. The Standard Conditions of Sale stipulate for a completion period of 10 business days once the notice to complete has been served. If the transaction is not completed by that time, then the seller can terminate the contract, retain the deposit, and start marketing the property again.

If, on the other hand, the seller is the party unable/unwilling to complete, then the buyer can serve a notice to complete and force the seller to complete within 10 business days. If the seller fails to do so, then the buyer can terminate the contract, request back the deposit plus interest, and potentially get compensation for the expenses associated with the transaction so far (e.g. legal fees, search fees, etcetera).

5. POST-COMPLETION

The legal representatives of both parties need to attend to a number of matters post-completion. While some of those might be done within a few days (i.e. passing the keys and paying SDLT), others will require the legal representative's immediate attention (i.e. redeeming the mortgage).

a. KEYS PASS TO THE BUYER

If the seller is using an estate agent, he will authorise the estate agent to pass the keys to the buyer. The agents will negotiate the exact time and date with the buyer.

If the seller is not using an estate agent, some arrangement should be achieved with the buyer.

b. MORTGAGE REDEMPTION

The mortgage will be redeemed at the time the legal representative received the proceeds of sale from the legal representative of the buyer. The redemption needs to take place on the day of completion and the money should be sent before 3:30PM, to ensure that the lender receives it on the same day.

The discharge of the mortgage takes place by submitting forms DS1[38] (for the discharge of the registered charge) or DS3[39] (for a release of a part of the registered estate from a registered charge). Those forms are not submitted independently. They must be accompanied by a form AP1[36] which is the general form that needs to be submitted when making changes to the register for a property.

Often the lender will take care of the administration of the discharge and submit the required forms. However, your legal representative should confirm this and inquire if there is any supplementary information that needs to be provided.

c. ESTATE AGENT FEES

The fees of the estate agent will have to be settled by the seller's legal representative from the proceeds of the sale. Usually, the agent would have sent their commission invoice after the exchange of contracts. The invoice should detail the payment timeline and amount.

d. STAMP DUTY LAND TAX

The buyer's legal representative needs to submit a SDLT return and pay the liability within 30 days of completion. There is a fine of £100 for not paying the SDLT liability on time.

The calculations of SDLT and the different forms that need to be completed were already discussed in Chapter 6. Upon payment, the legal representative of the buyer will be issued with a Land Transaction Return Certificate (form SDLT5). This is a confirmation of the payment of SDLT to HMRC concerning the specific property transaction.

While the legal deadline for paying the liability is 30 days, at this stage the legal representative of the buyer would have given the lender an undertaking to make all necessary SDLT payments to HMRC within a specified period from the completion. This period may very well be shorter than 30 days, with some lenders requiring the SDLT payment to be made within a week of completion. The lender would also require for the proof of payment, SDLT5, to be provided at least 10 days before the expiration of the priority period of the OS1[31] or OS2[32] Land Registry search (discussed in Chapter 6).

The lender would require such an undertaking, because the SDLT5 form needs to be included with the Land Registry application. We already discussed the significance of the OS1[31]/OS2[32] priority period in Chapter 6. The priority period ensures that nobody else can register an interest over the property in that period. As a result, the lender would want to register the mortgage over the property before the period expires. Missing the priority period would mean that another lender could register a first mortgage over the property.

e. EXECUTION OF SHARE TRANSFERS

As already explained in Chapter 4, the owners of a property might be a part of an association that manages the common areas of a building. As a result, when purchasing the interest from the owner, the buyer is becoming member of the association. Usually, such associations are private limited companies and the buyer will become a member only after he acquires the requisite shares from the seller. For the purpose, the seller will have to sign a stock transfer form and give that to the buyer alongside the share certificates. Normally, such a transaction will incur a Stamp Duty tax of 0.5%, however the seller will make a special declaration in the stock transfer form for the buyer to be exempt from paying Stamp Duty on the transfer of shares. Then the buyer will send the stock transfer form and the share certificates to the company he is becoming a shareholder of. In response, the association will have to issue new share certificates to the buyer of the property within two months and will register the buyer on its register of members. As a result, the buyer becomes a shareholder of the commonhold/leasehold association that is managing the common areas of the building.

f.   LAND REGISTRY REGISTRATION APPLICATION

Once the purchase is completed, the buyer's legal representative will have to register the transfer. A few different forms are needed for this to take place. It is important to complete the registration within the priority period of the OS1[31]/OS2[32] search conducted. Just like in the case of the mortgage registration described above, you must complete the registration while you have the security that no third party can register any interest over the property being purchased.

Form AP1[36], which was already referenced in the preceding paragraphs, should be included. This form is a general application to change the register.

Additionally, the transfer deeds will have to be submitted at the Land Registry. The seller's legal representative would have executed the form (TR1[25]or TP1[26]) as a deed and posted it to the buyer's legal representative after receiving the completion funds. The form was discussed in Chapter 6.

The buyer's legal representative will also have to enclose the fee payable to the Land Registry. For the purposes, the Land Registry has made available a calculator tool[39] that allows for the quick calculation of the fee based on the value of the property and the type of transaction. The fee can be paid by cheque or postal order. It can also be made using a credit/debit card or cash, if you make an appointment at a local Land Registry office.

The Land Registry has a portal that can be used to make the payment. Professional firms might have Business Gateway integrated into their case management system, which would allow for another way of paying the fees online.

There is a substantial discount if the land registration fee is paid online. The government has published the relevant fees on their website[40]. There are two schedules for fees: Schedule 1 and Schedule 2. For a transaction involving registered land and consideration, the relevant fees are in Schedule 1. For a gift of land, for example, the relevant fees are in Schedule 2.

If, for example, you buy a registered property for £450,000, then the fee will be: £270 for an application by post and £135 for an application through the portal or Business Gateway.

g. REGISTRATION AT COMPANIES HOUSE

If a company purchases the property, then the legal mortgage over the property will have to be registered at Companies House Beta[35]. For this, form MR01[41] and a copy of the instrument creating the mortgage will have to be sent to the Companies House, alongside the appropriate fee. For a paper application, at the time of writing this the fee is £23. Companies that are registered for Web-Filing can use the web portal[42] to register the charge. In that case, the required fee is only £15. Those fees are correct as of the time of writing of this book.

h. MISCELLANEOUS

At this stage, there might be a few minor questions to attend to. The seller will have to notify all tenants, if there are any, about the change of ownership and provide them with the new bank details for the payment of rent. If the buyer has chosen a different deposit protection scheme, the tenant's deposit should be transferred to the new scheme.

The seller should examine the meters in the property and record the final measures just before completion. Those expenses will be apportioned, as discussed above.

When the Land Registry sends the buyer the title information document, the details should be confirmed to ensure no mistakes were made.

Additional questions might arise that are specific to your transactions. However, at this point the transaction is completed and you can congratulate yourself for completing a successful purchase/sale.

CHAPTER EIGHT
Additional Considerations

While the sale has officially been completed, there are number of general areas of concern that a buyer/seller should be mindful of.

1. UNDERTAKINGS

Throughout the sale process we referenced undertakings on numerous occasions. The seller's legal representative had to give an undertaking on form TA13[18] that the mortgage over the property will be redeemed with the proceeds of the sale. The buyer's legal representative had to give an undertaking to the lender that the SDLT will be paid to HMRC within the specified period. Furthermore, both legal representatives had to give numerous undertakings in the process of exchanging contracts over the telephone. They had to undertake to send their signed part of the contract to the opposing party by the end of the day. At that point, the buyer's legal representative also had to undertake that he would send the deposit with the signed contract.

Since undertakings play a crucial role in residential property transactions, it is important to examine what constitutes an undertaking and what makes it enforceable.

Generally, undertakings are promises to do something. A crucial element of determining whether a promise is an undertaking is whether the benefiting party placed any reliance on it. Undertakings do not have to contain the word "undertaking" or to be in writing. However, including the word undertaking and a specific time frame increase the chances that the court will interpret the promise as an undertaking. An undertaking must be discharged within the time period specified, or, if no such period is given, within a reasonable time.

Of course, not every promise is legally binding. If your legal representative promised the opposing side to give them a call and discuss the terms of the contract, not calling them would not be a breach of undertaking.

The context of the promise will be very important. If the promise is given as a part of the standard procedure of exchange of contracts over the telephone, in accordance with the formulas provided by the Law Society and discussed in Chapter 5, this will clearly be interpreted as an undertaking.

Similarly, form TA13[18] makes it very clear that the answers to two of the questions on the form, relating to completion by post and the redemption of the seller's mortgage, will be interpreted as undertakings.

Next, we must examine what the consequences are for not fulfilling an undertaking. A court action can be commenced against a legal representative that has failed to comply with an undertaking. For example, a legal representative will undertake to redeem the mortgage in response to question 5.2 of form TA13[18]. However, if he sends the sale proceeds to the seller instead, the court will hold the legal representative personally liable for discharging the mortgage.

There are two main avenues to enforce an undertaking. A civil action claim for breach of contract can be commenced against the legal representative. The court will award specific performance of the undertaking or damages.

The other route is to inform the Solicitors Regulation

Authority[43] (SRA) and the Solicitors Disciplinary Tribunal[44] (SDT). While the SRA and SDT cannot enforce undertakings, a breach will lead to professional sanctions and fines.

Finally, the High Court[45] has an inherent jurisdiction over all solicitors, as officers of the court, and can compel them to comply with an undertaking or to pay compensation.

2. FRAUD

The high price of real estate nowadays means that the parties are often obliged to transfer substantial amounts of money. This makes property transactions an enticing prospect for fraudsters.

a. THIRD PARTY FRAUD

One possible scheme for committing fraud involves communicating the wrong bank details. The legal representative of the seller is usually very careful when communicating the account information to the legal representative of the buyer. This is because it may be possible for a third party to intercept the message and change the account details. This can happen whether it is being send by e-mail or post. As a result, the seller's legal representative would transfer the monies to the wrong the bank account. In this situation, the buyer will still be expected to complete the purchase and will have to find additional funding to cover the outstanding amount on the transaction.

Expert's View

There have been cases where someone from the post room was involved in the fraud. They intercepted the Requisitions on Title, changed the bank details and then posted the letter to the buyer's solicitor. Luckily, the buyer's solicitor examined the form. The document didn't seem to be type properly, so he called to double-checked the bank details. Then it transpired that the details were falsified and tampered with. That is why it is always good practice to double-checking the bank details that are stated in the Requisition on Title, whether it was sent through e-mail or post.

I have now adopted a policy whereby I no longer send out my client account details in open emails. My system may be security protected, but a fraudster can intercept a client's email from their generic account. I will utilise the following methods to send the client account details:

1. *Sending an encrypted PDF zip file and I will confirm the password to the client by telephone and text.*
2. *By telephone.*
3. *By text (and usually with a follow up telephone call)*

From a buyer client perspective, it is always best to verify bank details with your solicitor over the telephone before making any transfers.

A seller client and their solicitor should do likewise, and verify the bank details for the sale proceeds over the telephone as well.

Another alternative is to have entirely encrypted emails between the solicitor and the client. However, this may be too costly for smaller firms to adopt. Therefore, the above simple steps will be appropriate. We need to get used to using traditional methods of communicating with each other again and not rely entirely on email.

Cindi Van Graan,
Sole-Practitioner Solicitor

b.   VENDOR FRAUD

Another possibility is that the legal representative of the seller is not a legitimate solicitor/conveyancer. The two legal representatives will be in constant contact, so it will be very difficult for the seller's supposed representative to sustain the deception for a long period of time. However, if he achieves that, the transaction money will be sent to the wrong bank account. Once again, the buyer will have to incur a substantial loss.

A possible way to prevent dealing with fraudulent vendors is to do a check on the bank account the seller's legal representative gives you. There are different search agents that will check whether the bank account has a track record of previous use in the residential property market. The check will also cross-reference the bank account and sort code with the name of the legal representatives and their postcode. Once you are satisfied that the account is legitimate and is frequently used for property transactions, you can be safe to proceed with the transaction.

c.   LENDER FRAUD

It is unlikely to experience mortgage fraud if you employ the services of a high-street bank. Those institutions abide by strict compliance procedures and are regulated by numerous government agencies.

However, it is important to ensure that your lender is an FCA[46] authorized lender and that the mortgage is compliant with the Council of Mortgage Lenders handbook[4]. Examining the mortgage for any unusual conditions like hidden fees and unreasonable interest rate increases is a very important for protecting the interest of the borrower.

d.   BORROWER FRAUD

There are several different ways for borrowers to commit fraud.

135

Some borrowers inflate their incomes in order to obtain larger loans at better interest rates. Submitting fake records or records that do not truly represent the buyer's regular income statements is typical for this type of fraud. For example, submitting income statements for the last 3 months of your lucrative work as a contractor would be a misrepresentation if you are fully aware that your contract is about to expire and you will not continue to receive such high income.

Another possible fraud would be to take out the mortgage under a different name, following identity theft. That is why it is important for legal representatives to perform all necessary identify checks as soon as the client first contacts them.

Overvaluing properties is another method for committing mortgage fraud. A borrower will be able to take out a larger loan if the lender is convinced that the collateral is more valuable than it actually is. That is why many lenders require a valuation survey to be conducted by a Chartered surveyor, as described in Chapter 1.

Deposit fraud is another possibility for committing mortgage fraud. A lender would usually require 10% of the purchase price to be financed by the borrower. That money cannot be a loan from another lender. The basic idea behind the 10% personal contribution required by the lender is that this will limit the overall leverage of the borrower and the transaction would pose less risk for the lender. For that purpose, the borrower must show proof of the source of the 10% deposit he is contributing. It is possible for buyers to borrow the deposit from another lender and then provide fake documents to prove the source of the deposit. Of course, this is a form of money laundering and is illegal.

e. REGISTRATION FRAUD

It is possible for someone else to register your property under his or her name. This is not only a risk at the time of buying/selling residential property, as it can happen at any time.

This may occur because of identity theft. People that do not live in the property are more likely to fall victim of such fraud. Not having a mortgage over the property also makes it easier to suffer registration fraud, as there will be no registered mortgages to discharge before registration by the new "owner".

Expert's View

Fraudsters go to great lengths to create forged documents to impersonate owners and will even have their names changed by Deed Poll in order to obtain identity documents which will have the effect of trying to satisfy a solicitor into believing their due diligence requirements have been met.

Sellers who let out their property or who leave it vacant for significant periods should undertake periodic checks. Some warning signs to look out for include:

» *If the property is tenanted ensuring you are dealing with the owner/landlord;*

» *There is no estate agent is involved, or an individual with no history of being an estate agent purports to be the seller's agent and is the only one giving instructions on behalf of the seller;*

» *If the seller is putting pressure on the buyer unreasonably, to complete quickly without any valid reason;*

» *If there are discrepancies between information being provided by the supposed seller and the property itself (in the descriptions, sale particular, and survey etc.) and no explanation can be provided by the seller as to the discrepancy;*

» *If the seller threatening to withdraw from the transaction where he is being asked to provide further information and replies to enquiries; and*

» *If the seller is consistently out of the country and/or unavailable.*

Cindi Van Graan,
Sole-Practitioner Solicitor

The increasing frequency of this type of fraud is starting to receive media attention. In its May 2017 article "Help! My house has been hijacked[47].", the Financial Times indicated that The Land Registry has prevented frauds on 254 registration applications since September 2009, representing a total property value of approximately £117 million. For such a scheme to succeed, the fraudster will have to rent out the property. Then they will change their name by a deed pool to the name of the legal owner of the property and place it on the market for sale. The tenants will usually attempt to put pressure on the legal representatives to complete the sale as soon as possible. Furthermore, they would target cash buyers, as lenders will conduct additional checks before releasing the mortgage funds.

Sometimes that type of fraud is detected at the point of registering the property at the Land Registry. However, the sale is completed by that point and the tenant has obtained the funds. It is often very difficult to trace the money or the fraudsters. The Land Registry would not allow a registration to take place in those circumstances. Even if the new owner manages to register the property, the previous owner can challenge that and get the property back. As a result, it is usually the buyer that suffers a loss.

It is possible for a buyer that has fallen victim to such fraud to sue their legal representative. The courts place an emphasis on the role that the legal representatives of the buyer and seller have played in the transaction and on any negligent acts they might have committed in the process of conveyancing. Whilst the courts may sometimes decide that the loss will have to be divided between the legal representatives of both sides, it appears that the legal representative of the buyer is the one that usually has to bear the burden.

This type of fraud is becoming more prevalent; with the Land Registry recording 50 attempts to change the land register fraudulently in the financial year 2016-2017. For those reasons the Land Registry is placing an emphasis on preventative action. It has created a notification system[48] that allows an owner to track any registrations relating to the property. If someone tries to change the register by registering a mortgage over your property, you will receive a notification. The system will alert you about any pending changes, however it will not automatically stop them. It will be your responsibility to contact the Land Registry property fraud line in case you are the victim of registration fraud.

It is also possible to put a restriction on the ability of the Land Registry to register a sale or a mortgage on your property. No such registration will be made, unless a solicitor or a conveyance certifies that you made the application.

3.   DELAYS

We have discussed the importance of delays on several occasions throughout the book. This is mainly due to the nature of residential property transactions, which contains a high volume of paperwork circulating between multiple parties.

Throughout the cycle of a property transaction, numerous bundles of documents must be sent to the buyer, the seller and the lender. Third parties like an estate agent, local council, or insurance provider are likely to be involved too. Naturally, if one party is slow in providing the required information, this will affect the full chain of communication.

a. EXAMPLES

A typical example would be, the legal representative of the buyer might not be able to send the Certificate of Title to the lender, because he has not yet received the Energy Performance Certificate from the estate agent of the seller. If the certificate is not available, the estate agents might have to commission one from a registered assessor, which delays the transaction even more. Only after the legal representative of the buyer obtains the certificate will the full Certificate of Title be sent to the lender. The minimum review period might vary from one to several weeks, and there is a possibility that the lender might find some aspects questionable and raise additional Pre-Exchange inquiries. This can delay the exchange of contract quite a bit

Another possible delay can be caused because the seller is not providing the buyer's legal representative with the building regulations certificates of completion. This might be the case, because he lost the certificates or because he never obtained them when buying the property in the first place. The seller can request from the council to issue replacement certificates, or if none were issued to begin with, to come and verify the safety of all building alterations. Alternatively, indemnity insurance could be put in place as discussed in Chapter 3. Naturally, this process might take a few weeks.

It is important to note that significant delays can require additional searches and visits to the property. If your first visit took place a few months ago, it is advisable to visit again to confirm whether any significant changes have taken place, whether any alterations took place and whether the condition of the property worsened. Furthermore, searches that took place several months ago might no longer be relevant, the council might have given permission for the construction of an office building in close proximity of the desired property.

Expert's View

If there is a long period between exchange and completion, the searches are likely to expire and must therefore be repeated. Additionally, a buyer might have to look at the property more than once. If there are only a couple of weeks between exchange and completion they need to visit the property only once to inspect it and measure it up. However, if the period between exchange and completion is longer – for example 3 months – the buyer may wish to should visit, say, once a month. The last visit should be a week before completion.

Cindi Van Graan,
Sole-Practitioner Solicitor

b.   CHAINS OF TRANSACTIONS

Similar delays are even more pronounced in chains of property transactions. There are more parties involved in such transactions and each one can cause delays similar to the ones observed in the scenarios above. Furthermore, the delays will cause frustration and loss to multiple parties. As a result, it is more difficult to navigate a chain of related property transactions.

c.   NEW-BUILDS

Conveyancing delays can be especially relevant in new-build properties. When buying new-builds, you are signing a contract for a property that is not completed, and possibly even not started. We already discussed in Chapter 2 that this would cause problems when obtaining a mortgage. Usually, a lender would be willing to provide a mortgage only three months before the completion of the new build. As a result, it is important to try and predict a number of elements, such as the property values at the time of completion, your future income, and other major future expenses a few years in advance.

This process can be complicated additionally by the usual delays that any construction process might undergo. The building company might be affected by lack of financing, adverse weather conditions, missing building permits and even a skilful labour shortage. It is important to receive regular updated from the selling agents about the progress of the building work.

Expert's View

The contracts for new builds stipulate that a 10-day notice for completion will be given. As a result, it is very important to have the funds for the transaction ready. If the construction work will take years, then it is advisable for the buyer's solicitor to inquire with the developer and their estate agent for estimates on the expected completion date. Some developers would have an office on site in order to provide information on the development.

I have not dealt with any developers who have agreed to a completion period longer than 10 working days from service of the notice to complete. Usually, there is no room for negotiation, as the developers would try to follow their schedule – for example all 50 houses on the left side of the development would complete within just a few days.

Cindi Van Graan,
Sole-Practitioner Solicitor

If a delay takes place, then party that is ready to complete can send the other party a Notice to Complete, we described the process and consequences of serving such a notice in Chapter 6. This gives the other party 10 business days to complete the transaction. It is important to mention that even if the offending party manages to complete in the given period, it will owe interest on the outstanding amount for the delay caused. The interest is calculated based on the completion date and the agreed contract rate.

The contract rate that can be found in the Standard Conditions of Sale is based on The Law Society's contract rate, which is 4% over the current Barclays Bank base rate. As of March 2017, the Barclays Bank base rate is 0.5%, which means the offending party will have to pay an annual interest of 4.5%.

For example, if the buyer, using the Standard Conditions of Sale, did not have the sufficient funds to complete on 1st April 2017, and instead was able to complete on 11th April 2017, interest of 4.5% per annum will be charged for 10 days. If the outstanding amount was £450,000, the resulting penalty would be: (£450,000 * 0.045 * 10)/365 = £550.

4. FEES

There are a number of fees incurred throughout the process of buying/selling residential property. Before completion, the legal representatives will send their clients a Completion statement, which was described in Chapter 7. This statement will give the client a detailed account of the different expenses incurred in the process.

a. LEGAL EXPENSES

The fees that the legal representatives charge their clients can be an area of concern for some buyer/sellers. Usually, the legal fee would be agreed upon up-front – before the conveyancing process even begins. It is important to ask your legal representative about the amount they will charge you for the transaction. With sale/purchase of residential property, legal representatives usually charge a fixed amount, as opposed to an hourly charge that is applicable in other types of cases. It is important to check if the quoted amount includes VAT. It is also important to discuss if this amount is subject to changes. If, for example, there are unpredicted complications in the conveyancing process and your representative will have to spend significantly more time on the transaction, they might be inclined to charge additional fees. However, those need to be negotiated and agreed with the client and cannot be unilateral, unannounced additional fee.

When discussing the price with your legal representative, it is advisable to ask about disbursements. Those are fees that the legal representative will have to pay to third parties throughout the transaction. Those can be fees for the register of title, a building survey, environmental search and chancel insurance, to name a few. It is advisable for you to agree on an approximate amount for such disbursements, in order to have a clear idea of what the final bill will be. Such an agreement would also mean that you should receive an update from your legal representative if the disbursements are surpassing the initial estimate.

The Completion Statement might include some additional legal fees, beyond the fees of your representative and the disbursements. One example of an additional fee is an engrossment fee. As described in Chapter 6, an engrossment of the transfer deed is prepared by one of the sides, according to the conditions of the contract. The engrossment of the deed constitutes an official final version of the deed, usually printed on special paper. Typically, legal representatives will charge about £150 plus VAT for engrossment.

Expert's View
Engrossment is simply agreeing and printing the

final version on thicker paper, binding it, and sending it out for execution. Unfortunately, it is common for engrossment fees to be charged to the buyer in new build transactions. The contract usually includes an engrossment prepared by the seller's solicitor, which is specified in the contract as being payable by the buyer. This is usually non-negotiable and the honest truth is that the seller's solicitor is not going to waive the fee. The buyer should expect their solicitor to inform them about such a fee in advance.

Cindi Van Graan,
Sole-Practitioner Solicitor

It is important to discuss the legal bills on the Completion Statement with your legal representative. Generally, your representative can charge legal fees only after reaching an agreement with you. If, for example, you see a charge for local council search amounting to £30 and a legal fee of £50 for requesting and reviewing the search results, you should raise the issue with your representative. This would amount to an additional professional fee that was not previously disclosed and agreed upon. It is best to negotiate whether you will accept any such additional charges that were accrued as a result of performing the expected work of a legal representative.

b. MORTGAGE EXPENSES

The Completion Statement of the buyer will contain a number of fees associated with the mortgage. Those fees will likely include a mortgage handling fee, which is a fee the legal representative will charge for working on the approval of the offer and any associated inquiries. One again, it is best to raise the issue of such additional fees in the very first meeting with the legal representative. It is important to have clarity whether such additional fees, for work performed by the legal representative, are acceptable. There will also likely be a telegraphic transfer fee, for transferring the money from the lender to the buyer's legal representative, and then to the seller's legal representative.

c. MISCELLANEOUS EXPENSES

The completion statement will contain charges relating to the payment of Stamp Duty Land Tax, which was described in detail in Chapter 6. This charge will depend on the value of the property and there is nothing that can be done about the sum. However, some legal representatives will include a Stamp Duty Land Tax handling fee, in a way similar to the fee for handling the mortgage offer. This is an expense that should have been disclosed and you can raise the issue with the legal representative.

You should also encounter an expense for registering the transfer at the Land Registry, which was described in detail in Chapter 7. This expense is fixed and based on the value of the property and type of application.

Another expense that might appear on the Completion statement, in the case of leasehold purchases, is the cost of LPE1[20]. As described in Chapter 2, the LPE1[20] is a form used to raise inquiries from the holders of the freehold estate. The seller of the leasehold will usually incur the cost, even though this is something that can be negotiated in the contract.

A similar expense in the sale of leasehold properties is the cost of a management pack. The buyer can request the leasehold owner to provide such a pack. The cost will usually be covered by the seller and will appear in the Completion Statement. It is good practice for the legal representative to raise those additional leasehold expenses when discussing the disbursements, as they can easily amount to several hundred pounds.

5.   INADEQUATE DUE DILIGENCE

As you know by now, the process of purchasing/selling a property is very complicated and involves a vast amount of exchange of information between multiple parties. As a result, it is conceivable that your legal representatives might make a mistake at some point of the process. Real estate transactions often involve considerable sums of money, so that mistake might cost you a lot of money. It is important to examine the courses of action you might take in such a situation.

The first step should be to contact your legal representative and explain the situation. He might suggest a solution that you will find satisfactory such as paying your local council fine, for example.

If you cannot reach an agreeable plan with your legal representative, you can contact the Legal Ombudsman. The Legal Ombudsman can award damages in cases of inadequate service. However, those are often limited in scope and will not compensate your full loss. Furthermore, if you accept the award offered by the Ombudsman, then agree not to bring the case against a court of law. Thus, this route should not be chosen for cases involving substantial loss.

The final course of action you should consider is litigation. If you experience problems due to the negligence of your legal representative, then you can initiate a civil action against him. If, for example, your legal representative never checked if a building regulation certificate was issued and the council has discovered the omission and has fined you, you may be able to sue your legal representative. If your legal representative missed that the title of the seller is possessory and subsequently another person with a better claim appears and claims the property, you may be able to sue your legal representative. If an environmental search was never conducted and the local authority locates mercury poisoning in the ground beneath your house and compels you to remediate the land, you may be able to sue your legal representative.

The first key element that you will need to prove when suing your legal representative is that he owed you a duty of care. You are owed that duty, because your legal representative is a vendor of professional services. This duty is owed throughout the transaction – when communicating and negotiating with the opposing legal representative, when examining search results, when completing the money transfer, etcetera.

The next step is to establish that the duty was breached. Describing the actions of your legal representative and how they differed from the actions of a reasonable professional in the same circumstances is critical for establishing the breach of the duty.

Then, you will need to prove that the breach of duty in question caused you a loss. Any of the actions described above (paying for remediation of the land, losing the property to someone with a better title, being fined by the local council for a missing building regulation certificate) will cause you financial loss, which will have to be shown in court.

The final step is to show that there was causation between the breach of duty by your legal representative and the loss you suffered. The loss cannot be too far removed from the breach and usually there cannot be any third parties intervening in the chain of causation.

You will undoubtedly need to engage solicitors, and they will be the ones that have to prove each one of the steps described above in the process of litigation against the legal representative who mishandled your property transaction. However, it is important that you understand the general requirements of such a case and the way to proceed in order for you to be aware of the strength of your claim.

On the next pages, we have included a summary of the main steps of the conveyancing process for your convenience.

Although the table provided does not include any of the details about the steps, you may find it useful as a guide to determine at which stage of the property purchase/sale you are currently at and what remains to be done.

Expert's View

While the following is not the one definitive way for a property transaction to proceed, most transactions follow those rough guidelines:

Pre-Exchange Preparation Checklist	
Seller/Seller's Solicitor	Buyer/Buyer's Solicitor
Accept buyer's offer and instruct solicitor	Make offer and instruct solicitor
Receives sales memo from estate agent	Receives sales memo from estate agent
Signs engagement documents, provides identity documents and completed protocol forms and any original property deeds	Signs engagement documents, provides identity documents, makes payment on account for search fees
	Buyer Progresses mortgage application and instructs survey/ valuation with lender
Solicitor confirms instruction to other firm	Solicitor confirms instruction to other firm
Draw up draft Contract, collate supporting documents including register entries, title plan, completed protocol forms and supporting documents referred to in protocol forms	
Request leasehold management pack/ Replies for form LPE1[20] (service charge and ground rent can be managed by separate agents which means separate packs must be obtained	

Send Contract pack to seller's solicitor	Review of Contract pack; leasehold enquiries; order property searches
If applicable - Request Licence to Assign from landlord	Review Licence to Assign
Amend and engross contract; raise enquiries with seller client and send replies to enquiries	Investigate title, make any necessary amendments to draft Contract; raise enquiries
	Survey report reviewed
	Order any other extra searches, planning, mining etcetera
Reply to any additional enquiries	Review property search results and raise any additional enquiries
	Receive mortgage offer and instructions and review
	Report any concerns to lender if applicable in accordance with CML Handbook and lender's own specific instructions
	Report to Buyer (on property and mortgage – sending mortgage deed for execution at that point)
	Carry out verification checks on seller's solicitor, using LawyerChecker https://www.lawyerchecker.co.uk/
Hold Signed Contract in readiness for exchange	Hold Signed Contract in readiness for exchange
	Buyer transfers Deposit Funds
If short period between exchange and completion request redemption statement	If short period between exchange and completion hold signed Mortgage Deed and send Certificate on Title to Lender
Approve draft Transfer	If short period between exchange and completion prepare draft Transfer
Agree completion date	Agree completion date

Take final instructions/authority from client	Take final instructions/ authority from client
EXCHANGE CONTRACTS	
Send seller part contract in post	Send Buyer part contracts in the post with deposit cheque (monies may have been held to order until completion)

Pre-Completion Preparation Checklist	
Seller/Seller's Solicitor	**Buyer/Buyer's Solicitor**
Approve Transfer Deed	Prepare Draft Transfer Deed
Reply to Requisitions on Title	Send out Requisitions on Title and ensure satisfactory replies received
Seller to execute approved Transfer Deed	Buyer to execute approved Transfer Deed if required (i.e. indemnity clause included)
Obtain Mortgage Redemption Statement	Buyer to execute Mortgage Deed
Obtain up-to-date ground rent, service charge receipts/demands to calculate apportionments	Prepare SDLT Return and arrange for signing
Prepare Completion Statement	Apply for pre-completion searches and ensure clear results
Seller to take final meter readings	Certificate of Title to lender in sufficient time
Prepare discharge forms (DS1[38]) if necessary for lender to execute and return after mortgage redemption	Review Completion Statement from seller's solicitor
If sale of buy-to-let prepare Rent Authority Letter to go to tenants instructing future rent to be made to buyer	Check with lender that funds will be received in time for completion
Collate completion Deeds and documents to be handed over to buyer on completion	Check whether any of the seller's warranties and insurance policies are to be assigned to buyer and prepare assignment documents

Check vacant possession (if not selling subject to tenancy) and how all keys are to be handed over (will agent be handed all keys for collection by buyer?)	Buyer to ensure appropriate life insurance arrangements in place as required by lender
Check when seller will actually vacate property – buyer may agree for seller to have more time to pack	Final Completion Statement/ Statement of Monies detailing any balance required from buyer to clear before completion (includes final bill)
Ensure estate agent is aware of completion date and any additional arrangements	Receive cleared mortgage funds from lender
Prepare Completion Statement to seller with final bill	Final inspection of property if necessary
	Check when property will be vacated and where (all) keys will be available for collection

Completion/Post-Completion Checklist	
Seller/Seller's Solicitor	Buyer/Buyer's Solicitor
Receive completion funds	Send completion funds
Confirm completion to Buyer's Solicitor	Inform Buyer of completion
Information seller of completion	Buyer collects keys from estate agent
Inform estate agent of completion and instruct to release keys	Complete the (Counterpart) Transfer Deed with the completion date
If onward purchase ensure sale proceeds sent on to seller's solicitor up the chain	Complete the Mortgage Deed with the completion date
Redeem existing mortgage	Submit SDLT Return and pay liability to HMRC (within 30 days)

Cancel existing buildings insurance policy	Register Legal Charge at Companies House within 21days if Buyer is a company
Sale proceeds transferred to Seller	Place any Indemnity Policies on Cover from the date of completion (if Seller has agreed to cover cost of premium ensure seller's solicitor places policy on cover)
Send DS1[38] (lenders discharge confirmation) to Buyer's solicitor if lender has not made electronic notification of discharge directly to HMLR	Check that discharge existing mortgage and confirm if DS1[38] or electronic notification to HMLR
Transfer tenants protected deposit or obtain release from scheme provider if buyer has set up deposit protection account with different scheme	Submit registration application to HMLR within priority search period (Land Registry Official Search (OS1[31]or OS2[32])
	Notice of transfer/ assignment and charge to landlord's solicitor within timescale specified in Lease (usually within 28/ 30 days from completion)
	Contact tenants to notify change of ownership and payment details of rent and protection of deposit
	Set up tenancy deposit protection if not already done
	Check title information document receive from Land registry following completion of registration to ensure no errors
	Agree arrangements for holding of any original deeds

Cindi Van Graan,
Sole-Practitioner Solicitor

REFERENCES

1. The Office for National Statistics:
www.ons.gov.uk

2. Mortgage Conduct of Business:
www.handbook.fca.org.uk

3. Affordable home ownership government scheme:
www.gov.uk/affordable-home-ownership-schemes

4. Mortgage Conduct of Business Rules:
www.handbook.fca.org.uk

5. The English Housing Survey:
www.gov.uk

6. Energy Performance Certificate:
www.gov.uk/buy-sell-your-home

7. Royal Institute of Chartered Surveyors:
www.rics.org/uk

8. Leasehold Reform Act 2002:
www.legislation.gov.uk

9. HSBC – cost of separate legal representation:
www.hsbc.co.uk

10. Law Society:
www.lawsociety.org.uk

11. Land Registry:
eservices.landregistry.gov.uk

12. Form OC1:
www.gov.uk

13. TA6:
www.lawsociety.org.uk

14. UKradon:
www.ukradon.org

15. TA7:
www.lawsociety.org.uk

16. TA9:
www.lawsociety.org.uk

17. TA10:
www.lawsociety.org.uk

18. TA13:
www.lawsociety.org.uk

19. The Standard Conditions of Sale (fifth edition):
www.lawsociety.org.uk/

20. LPE1:
www.lawsociety.org.uk

21. Matrimonial home rights:
www.legislation.gov.uk

22. Coal Authority:
www.gov.uk

23. HS2 web-page:
www.gov.uk/check-hs2-route

24. The Law Society:
www.lawsociety.org.uk

25. TR1:
www.gov.uk

26. TP1:
www.gov.uk

27. STLD Calculator:
www.tax.service.gov.uk

28. Online services:
www.gov.uk

29. Guide for SDLT1 form:
www.gov.uk

30. SDLT repayment form:
www.gov.uk

31. OS1:
www.gov.uk

32. OS2:
www.gov.uk

33. K16:
www.gov.uk

34. K19:
www.gov.uk

35. Companies House Beta:
beta.companieshouse.gov.uk

36. AP1:
www.gov.uk

37. Landlord and Tenant (Covenants) Act 1995:
www.legislation.gov.uk

38. DS1:
www.gov.uk

38. DS3:
www.gov.uk

39. Land Registry calculator tool:
landregistry.data.gov.uk

40. Land Registry registration fees:
www.gov.uk

41. MR01:
www.gov.uk

42. Companies House web-filing portal:
ewf.companieshouse.gov.uk

43. Solicitors Regulation Authority:
www.sra.org.uk

44. Solicitors Disciplinary Tribunal
www.solicitorstribunal.org.uk/

45. High Court:
www.judiciary.gov.uk

46. FCA:
www.fca.org.uk

47. Lucy Warwick-Ching, *The Financial Times*, Help! My house has been hijacked, 12th May 2017:
www.ft.com

48. Property alert system:
propertyalert.landregistry.gov.uk

AFTERWORD

The main purpose of Buy or Sell Your Home: Legal Essentials for Smoother Property Transactions is to give a broad overview of the topics that might affect any residential property transaction. Given the complexity and ever-evolving nature of the law it is not possible to tackle in depth all the specific issues that you may encounter. Whatever your legal issue, it is always advisable to consult a legal professional for specialist, tailored advice.

ABOUT THE AUTHOR

Lucy attended the `Stella Maris' Convent school in North Devon, UK, and later moved to Australia to complete her degree and graduate studies in business management. She majored in Marketing with a module in Tax Law, which inspired her to go on and pursue Law further. She registered at Australian Graduate School of Management (ASGM) in Australia and completed a post-graduate in business management.

Lucy returned to the UK and completed a Graduate Diploma in Law and Legal Practice Course. After qualifying, she practiced in civil and property litigation and later broadened her legal repertoire to include commercial residential property and immigration matters. After this Lucy moved on to specialising in Business law.

The next stage in Lucy's legal journey was as an In-House solicitor to iconic fashion shoe designer, Jimmy Choo, OBE, becoming the family business advisor and solicitor to Jimmy Choo himself in 2009. Before long her hard work and professionalism also saw her found and become a partner in a London law firm. Since resigning from the firm in June 2015, Lucy has dedicated herself to Law Understood Ltd, whose dual aim is the promotion of the UK legal sector, and the publication of guidebooks on key legal issues and topics, which make the law readily accessible to business-owners and the general public alike.

Additionally, over the decades she has purchased, renovated and sold residential and commercial properties and let out several properties of her own both here and overseas.

From a business point of view, Lucy's academic and professional background has given her a great and detailed understanding of what it means to open up a business from scratch, and of all the ensuing complications of setting up, hiring staff, and leasing properties. She realises that for both the legally qualified, and especially for the layperson, the law can seem infinitely complex and daunting; which is why she set out to develop a guide covering the whole process of residential property conveyancing. Hopefully, this book will unravel many of the mysteries enshrouding the process of buying/selling a property in the UK.

Finally, on a personal note, Lucy is interested in fundraising for charities, helping others and empowering others to help themselves. She is a committee member of the Lawyers' Circle that works to raise much-needed funds for women in third world countries. In her spare time, she enjoys entertaining, and one day would like to be on 'Come Dine with Me'.

CONTRIBUTORS' BIOGRAPHIES

Andrew Kay
Arkade Property

Andrew is one of the founding directors and shareholders of Arkade Property, a residential and commercial sales and lettings agency. He currently heads the commercial property department, which deals with the sale and letting of commercial property and the sale and acquisition of businesses as a going concern. Andrew was educated at Solihull School and studied law at Manchester University (1979 – 1982,) where he was awarded the International Law prize, and Chester Law College (1982 – 1983) before joining Blakemores Solicitors in 1983. He subsequently joined Sydney Mitchell Solicitors where he became a partner, specialising in residential and commercial property law.

Cindi Van Graan
Protea Solicitors

Cindi has nearly a decade of legal experience in residential and commercial property transactions. Starting her career at a London law firm, specialising in property and commercial litigation. Cindi quickly rose through the ranks from paralegal to partner. In 2015 she established Protea Solicitors, a boutique law firm located in the West End of London. The motto of Protea Solicitors is People – Property – Passion. The firm is renowned for providing a personal and bespoke service, which means the stresses of a transaction are removed; decisive advice is provided; and the client is educated along the way.

Daniel Innes
Clear Insurance Group

Daniel has been an insurance broker for over 20 years. He began his career advising private clients on household and motor insurance after joining a small high street broker in Dulwich. In 2001 Dan moved to Clear Insurance, a new brokerage firm that has grown from a small firm of 12 to a business with four offices and 150 staff. Dan has looked after all types and sizes of client from one-man bands up to large listed companies. Now sitting on the Clear Insurance Board, Dan has responsibility for the commercial insurance division but still retains a client-facing role.

Malcolm Marsdin
Malcolm Marsdin and Company
Malcolm is a Chartered Surveyor and Registered Valuer based in Central London and specialises in residential surveys and valuations throughout Greater London. He qualified as a Chartered Surveyor in 1980 and set up his own Practice in 1985 - Malcolm Marsdin and Company.

Mathew Kind
The Kind Group
Mathew has over 15 years of experience in insurance, lending, banking, sales, marketing and recruitment. After spending 7 years at the local branch of a distinguished international bank, rising to the rank of branch manager, Mathew founded the Kind group with the goal of providing a wide-range of financial services in Birmingham and across the UK. After 12 years, the group includes: Kind Financial Services – specializing in Mortgages, Protection, home insurance, and business protection; Kind Consultancy – specializing in recruitment within Governance Risk & Compliance, Banking & Financial Services & Cyber Security; Kind Commercial – A Commercial Finance Brokerage and Kind Wealth – specializing in providing expert financial advice for Pensions & Investments specifically tailored to the needs of individuals & businesses.

Michael Connelly
iCompile Searches

Michael is a founding Director at iCompile Searches and has an intrinsic knowledge of market workings. Having seen numerous phases of the property search industry, Michael is confident of the future of it holds and has a strong belief in the fundamental approach, which has been adopted by private entities, working in this tough sector. Michael's core beliefs are based around integrity, hard work and a real belief in the product and this has driven the success of his business as one of the leaders in the market place, creating a nationally recognised brand in the property search market.

Paul Raglan
Mining Searches UK

A geologist, Paul has nearly 30 years' experience providing mining risk assessment reports nationwide.

Paul's specialist area of expertise lies with the metalliferous mining region of The South West of England where his company Mining Searches UK has been providing consultancy services for nearly 40 years.

From his unique and extensive digitised mine archive as well as specialist advice in site investigation and securing of mining features Paul has been providing solutions for developers in areas of former mining activity and his company is a leading provider of mining searches for the conveyancing market.

Paul has acted as an expert witness for contentious legal cases relating to historical mining activity and can be found talking at industry conferences.

Philip Li
DKLM LLP

Philip qualified as a solicitor in 1994 and is one of the four founding partners of DKLM. He specialises with non-contentious commercial and residential property transactions to include the acquisition and sale of all types of businesses, purchase and sale of portfolio investments, site acquisitions for development and new build off plan purchases. Philip has extensive links with the Chinese community in London. He regularly organises and speaks at investment seminars both in the UK and China. He is a member of the 48 Group and the China-Britain Business Council (CBBC) and an active member of the London Chinatown Lions Club and the Hong Kong Association.

Robert Wright
The Robinson Jackson Group
Robert began his career in property in 1997 as a weekend assistant and worked his way up, rising through the ranks and learning every aspect of estate agency. He deeply believes that property is more than bricks and mortar: it is about people. Robert opened his own estate agency in 2005, as part of the Robinson Jackson Group. Robinson Jackson is an award-winning Estate Agency that has been a market leader for over 50 years; it has 30 branches and departments in Kent and London. It is renowned for its first-class customer service and for the achievement of outstanding results through a positive attitude and hard-work.